A labyrinth in action at the Kirkridge Retreat Center, Bangor, PA, during a retreat led by the author.

The labyrinth is an ancient symbol that has been perceived as a metaphor of our lives. Each of us is on a journey towards finding our sacred center and achieving wholeness. The labyrinth is not a maze; it is not meant to trick the journeyer. Rather, it reminds the journeyer that each of us travels a unique path in life which often includes several twists and turns that ultimately lead to new discoveries. The labyrinth as featured on our cover includes the Star of Bethlehem and the birth of Christ. It leads to the center which represents Christ and life eternal for those who seek first the kingdom of God and His righteousness.

Pictured here is a real life labyrinth in action as participants of a retreat group make their personal pathway to the center. Here they will deposit a prayer or record their spiritual reflections. These discoveries surface during contemplative moments walking prayerfully toward the center. When their visit to the center is completed, the participants seek to find their way back to the starting point. The group gathers together later to share their insights and new directions contemplated in their life pilgrimages.

DISCOVERING

IN A

WORLD OF

UNCERTAINTY

REV. DR. WILLIAM W. MATZ, SR.

EDITED BY CAROL FEILBACH OLZINSKI

All profits from the sale of this book will be donated to three entities that have been significant to the author's faith formation:

- SCHOLARSHIP ASSISTANCE FOR STUDENTS
AT MORAVIAN THEOLOGICAL SEMINARY

- SPRUCE LAKE RETREAT CENTER'S
FOUNDATION FOR OUTDOOR MINISTRIES
TO ASSIST CHILDREN AND YOUTH IN NEED

- THE SALVATION ARMY FOOD PANTRY
OF BETHLEHEM, PA

To order additional copies, please contact us.
BookSurge
www.booksurge.com
1-866-308-6235

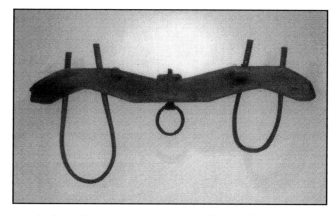

The yoke symbolizes those who have been the burden bearers of this book.
This yoke is housed at the Moravian Theological Seminary, Bethlehem, PA.

— ACKNOWLEDGEMENTS —

FROM THE AUTHOR

- The stories that appear in this book have been adapted from their rightful forms which appeared as monthly columns in the Spiritual Journey section of the Easton *Express-Times* newspaper.

- "Prayer Thoughts" found in the Reflection/Quest pages of each article are used by permission and drawn from selected sections of liturgies and hymns found in the *Moravian Book of Worship* of the Moravian Church in the U.S., 1995, unless otherwise noted. Other sources are individually noted and drawn from the New Revised Standard Version of the Bible.

SPECIAL THANKS TO THE FOLLOWING PEOPLE
WHO HELPED MAKE THIS BOOK POSSIBLE

- Carol Feilbach Olzinski, for her inspiration from beginning to end, and important contributions to the contents of the book

- To the ever-faithful and skilled print composer and designer, Donna Becker

- To my niece, Ann Greenzweig, in her skilled computer achievements and endless hours of reading my handwriting successfully

- My ready-to-go photographer and inspired poet, Dr. Arthur Freeman, and candid photographer John Mueller

- To our artist, Linda Orth, for her outstanding graphics

- To Gloria Conrad, Administrative Assistant, and the faculty, staff, and students of Moravian Theological Seminary for their ongoing partnership and love

- Jane Burcaw for important clues and guidance in getting started

- Overwhelming thanks to the countless caregivers and partners of my childhood and youth at the Ebenezer congregation

- To Deanna Hollenback, Editor of the *Moravian Magazine*, for pictorial permissions and advice

- David Bennett for supplying the finger labyrinth that inspired the front cover

- Particular gratitude to the local newspaper readers who through the years have expressed uplifting comments to me by personal contact, telephone calls, letters and emails

- An overwhelming cheer for the joyful and creative parishioners who encouraged me in the shepherding of the sheep: New Hartford, NY; Palmyra, NJ; Tuscarawas, OH; Lititz, PA; and Edgeboro, Bethlehem, PA

- To Susan Frantz of the Northampton Community College Duplication Center for the early enthusiasm she provided to me as I contemplated publishing this book

- To David Sanders, Sr., proprietor of Lumps Deli for his ready enthusiasm in discussing issues contained in this book while he served delicious hoagies and tasty cheese steaks

FROM THE EDITOR

- To my family: Your patience and support make everything I do possible. Thank you.

- Nate, Grace, and Sarah: Always dream big, play hard, and love God with all your heart!

- Dream-keeper: You are always in my thoughts and prayers.

– DEDICATION –

We dedicate this book to our family who were present for many of the
vacation experiences cited in the stories within these pages and in recognition of
our benevolent sons, Bill and Randy; their wives, Cindy and Debbie; and
our grandchildren: Jenny, Chelsea, Brandon, and Ashley.

The Matz Family on one of their many vacations together in numerous settings:
This one in Nova Scotia
First row left to right: Mary, wife; Jenny, Ashley, Chelsea, Bill, Jr.
Second row: Bill, Sr., the author; Brandon, Cindy, Debbie and Randy

— CONTENTS —

CHAPTER I

GOD'S LOVE

Creates

PAGE 1

CHAPTER II

GOD'S LOVE

Promises

PAGE 15

CHAPTER V

THE CERTAINTY OF

God's

Triumph

PAGE 129

CHAPTER VI

Seasonal Emphases

PAGE 143

ADVENT
CHRISTMAS
EPIPHANY
LENT
EASTER
PENTECOST

– FOREWARD –

This book reminds us of a marvelous truth: Each day, the promises of God's love are available to ordinary people – like you and me – in ordinary places. Eating in a restaurant, taking a walk in a park, fishing with a child; these are places where God's loving presence can be felt. Open your heart, seek Him, and you will be graced with His extraordinary response!

The stories presented in this book, along with their associated workbook pages, will assist you in considering your relationship with God thus far. Journal about your discoveries or even share them with others in a small group setting. I guarantee you that your "travels," whether alone or together with others, will be rewarding.

Carol Feilbach Olzinski

Carol is currently pursuing graduate degrees in Pastoral Counseling and Social Work from Moravian Theological Seminary and Marywood University, with a special interest in trauma, resiliency, and women's issues. She holds a Master's degree in American history from the University of Delaware, and a Bachelor's degree with a dual major in history and psychology from Cedar Crest College. She has taught history as an adjunct instructor at Northampton Community College, Bethlehem, Pennsylvania. Carol attends St. Peter's Evangelical Lutheran Church, Pen Argyl, Pennsylvania, where she is involved in youth ministry. She and her husband Brian are the parents of three children: Nathaniel, Grace, and Sarah.

"Discovering Promise in a World of Uncertainty" is based on sound theology and contemporary reality. This is a rare publication that manages to successfully intertwine devotion, reflection and life application while encouraging self-examination and hope-filled questioning. Its supportive and forgiving focus uplifts even as it challenges the reader to reach greater heights of self awareness and life application as a Christian and deeper depths of faith and connection to the God of our ancestors. This book is a perfect candidate for individual daily devotions, as a small group study guide, or as a discussion guide for youth and adult church school. The fact that the author is a Moravian and a personal friend of 18 years gives me greater joy as I recommend this positive, versatile and unusual devotional study.

Hopeton Clennon

Hopeton Clennon was elected a Bishop in the Moravian Church in 1998. He currently serves as Chaplain of Moravian College and Theological Seminary in Bethlehem, Pennsylvania. After his ordination in 1983, Hopeton served as a pastor in Jamaica, Washington, DC, Pennsylvania and California.

DISCOVERING
Promise
IN A WORLD OF UNCERTAINTY

– AN INTRODUCTION –

od desires to be in relationship with us – His creation. But day-to-day concerns and larger life crises lead many of us away from His nurturing hold. Sadly, a few of us even claim to have never truly known Him, while others choose to deny that God even exists. But, regardless of where we stand in our relationship with God, we all share in the struggle to remain hopeful about the future, especially in the midst of the uncertainty and pervasive cynicism that characterizes our current age.

Anxiety about our personal lives and the world at large causes a few to seek to escape the hard realities of life in various ways, including addictions, consumerism, and workaholism; many others actively seek answers to the questions that often overwhelm us but eventually opt to abandon the search: What will become of humankind as morality continues to decline? Will widespread environmental destruction and human suffering continue unabated? Is peaceful co-existence a lost cause? How will I care for my family if I lose my job or become seriously ill? Are my children safe? Can I truly trust anyone? The questions can seem daunting.

As a result, we need to seek out good news stories – faith stories – that will build us up rather than tear us down. We live in a world where bad news stories come at us from every angle. Every time we read the newspaper, check the internet, or watch television, we find ourselves swimming in bad news – stories about crime and mayhem – stories about bankruptcies and people out of work. But there are other stories out there – stories of faith triumphing over adversity – stories of people helping people – stories of parents raising children in the way that they should go. These are the good stories that we need to hear; we need to be reminded that God is still at work in the world and that God will ultimately triumph!

That's why this book may be for you. It is also ideal for youth and adult discussion groups in your community, places of worship, and even academic and work settings. Reflecting on the Bible or other sacred writings with others can be especially beneficial. It permits us to learn from other people of faith and to share in our commonly held struggles. When we rub shoulders with other spiritual searchers, we can provide encouragement to each other as we seek "a place to stand" on the challenging journey of life while living in the fervent hope that God's love ultimately will triumph.

This book is written for the believer who is struggling to "keep the faith" in the face of the abundant uncertainty that characterizes the human condition – as well as for those who cannot claim to have ever had it. While its approach is Christian, its contents are relevant for all faith traditions and philosophies. It contains a compilation of brief reflective stories regarding true life episodes that point to something that we can be certain of regardless of where we stand in our faith journey: the promise of God's unconditional love and presence revealed in ordinary places among ordinary people.

It is our hope that these brief stories will lead you to reflect on your faith journey and to consider actions you might take to grow more confident in God's promises. Fostering our spiritual lives requires discipline and a willingness to remain open to the work of God in our lives. God calls us, His creation, to stand-up under the pressures and uncertainties of the world, and to shine as hope-filled light into those all too familiar dark places. This work requires the sustaining love and power of God working within our hearts. The journey can be rough-going, but the sights along the way are sure to please and the final destination is without measure. God promises.

Author and Editor,

Bill and Carol
July 2009

– ABOUT THE AUTHOR –

Bill Matz has been seen "as a man for all seasons" and in a similar view is his wife Mary. It all began in Bethlehem, Pennsylvania, where he was nurtured in a warm Christian family of faith. His family was part of Ebenezer Mennonite Brethren in Christ congregation which provided endless leadership opportunities within youth programs and activities consisting of camping, retreats, ball teams, and establishing a Sunday school and developing service projects in a community low-income housing project.

Rev. Dr. Bill Matz

Following graduation from a vocational high school, he was drafted as a conscientious objector into the U.S. Army medical corps in World War II. He served in North Africa, Belgium, and Germany, tending to those battered in battle who experienced loss of limbs. These experiences helped to develop in him a world view and a growing call to enter the ordained ministry.

Bill returned from the service to engage in a 14-year higher education path including a degree at Moravian College, a Master's degree from Moravian Theological Seminary, and a Th.M. degree from Princeton Theological Seminary.

Later years provided the opportunity to pursue Ph.D. studies at Temple University and the achievement of a Doctor of Ministry degree from Drew University Graduate School of Religion.

Bill's 20 years of pastoral parish service began in organizing a new congregation in New Hartford, New York, followed by parishes in New Jersey, Ohio and Pennsylvania. He followed a call to

Rev. Dr. Mary Matz

serve as Dean of Moravian Theological Seminary for 17 years, during which the Seminary tripled in enrollment and multiplied new degree offerings to broaden the areas of service of its graduates serving on four continents of the globe.

During 15 years of post-retirement service, Bill has been engaged in teaching as an adjunct faculty member of both Moravian College and Northampton

Community College within the Philosophy Department. He teaches courses in ethics and moral problems, including On Death and Dying, World Religions, and Introduction to Philosophy.

Beyond parish and academic duties, Bill has also served within a variety of community, regional, and national agencies and endeavors. The Alumni Association of Moravian Theological Seminary has awarded Bill and his wife Mary the John Hus Award for excellence in ministry. Dr. Mary Matz was the first Moravian woman ordained in North America in the Moravian Church. Together they have provided a cumulative total of 87 years of ordained service. They are the parents of two sons: Bill, Jr. married to Debbie, and Randy married to Cindy. They have four grandchildren: Brandon, Ashley, Jenny and Chelsea.

– How To Read This Book –

A megalith gateway arch stands ready for visitors to the
Columncille Retreat Center, Bangor, PA.

1   Read in dialogue with the stories, insights and relevant scripture sources
    provided in each article, one at a time. Don't try to read the whole book in
    one or two sittings.

2   Allow the Bible to be a primary source, stimulating thought and worship as a
    tool for individual daily or weekly devotions, or for group study and activities.

3   Keep in mind that this book is intended to inspire as a comforting guide,
    not to solve all the problems of the reader's life and/or world.

4   See the book as a MAP . . . in the right direction.

5   Note that the themes set forth in the pages are truths, that the author has
    come to realize, because they are his or her experiences; however they are
    not limited to the author alone. There is no intention that this Study Guide
    imposes the writer's view on the readers.

6   For study and classroom groups, a prior preparation is *paramount.* The Reflection Page is there to assist you in reviewing basic questions for starters.

    a.   The Related Scripture Sources are designed to draw upon the Bible sources to introduce themes that emerge in digesting the article.

    b.   New Perspectives is intended to cause the reader to personally take a new step or embark in a new direction which engages salient truths brought into focus.

    c.   Unresolved Questions is to make everyone aware that exploring truths may not only stimulate faith in action but can also introduce some unexplored question for an in-depth review.

7   Start a study group using this book to encourage individuals to put their faith into action.

8   Enjoy finding God in common places.

Note

For literary ease of reading God has been referenced to in the masculine gender throughout this book. It is the author's hope that the reader recognizes that God in His awesomeness is gender inclusive.

Chapter I

God's Love

Creates

The first chapter of a book can be like a new dawn presenting a gift of fresh beginnings. Jesus likened the Spirit of God to the wind. It blows where it wishes, and "so it is with everyone who is born of the Spirit." (John 3.8) We see the effects of the Spirit of God in our lives. We hear the Spirit of God in the words of His people, and in His word and work. The Spirit of God can come to people in many ways, yet the effect is the same: A new birth which God creates. The Good News is that Christ can live in you and me!

The symbol above expresses the three basic components of the Good News: The Word (John 1:1), the World (John 3:16), and the Cross of Love (John 3:16).

A WAKE-UP CALL

Most of us experience at least one wake-up call in our life, when suddenly we see life and ourselves with new eyes. It may come in the form of a crisis, a thoughtful act, or just quiet reflection. For me it came one Sunday morning, as I was greeting people at the door of the church at which I was serving as pastor. The usual policeman was directing traffic outside, when I heard him excitedly call and gesture at a departing car to stop on the little lane between the church and the parsonage which was next door. I rushed to the scene to discover our son, three years of age, beneath the car. He had crawled through the hedge unnoticed by the driver. The front wheel of the car had pinched his leg and his forehead was bloodied. As I picked him up from under the car, the police cruiser pulled up and placed us inside as we hurried to the hospital.

As I held him and surveyed his body, appraising the seriousness of the injuries, I could hear the police officer radioing the hospital to alert them to our circumstances and advising doctors and an emergency crew to be available. A thousand images rushed through my mind. Gradually one question dominated, "Was I willing to give him up?"

While ultimately the injuries did not have destructive after-effects for our son with the exception of some leg scars, I know that I would never want to go through such an experience again. But, oddly enough, I also know that I would not want to be without the experience. You see, the event and the trauma had transformed how I perceived my role as a father.

From a spiritual perspective, I was awakened to a new perspective on an important truth conveyed in the Scriptures. John's Gospel states, "For God so loved the world that He gave His only Son, so that everyone who believes in Him may not perish but have eternal life." (3:16) This passage has been called "the Gospel in a Nutshell." It speaks of the nature of God's love at the conclusion of a very unique encounter between Jesus and a fascinating member of the "Who's Who of Jerusalem," a man of impeccable credentials by the name of Nicodemus. This man was a member of the Sanhedrin, the exclusive council which controlled the religious life of Israel. He was curious about Jesus because of all that had been happening. He stated to Jesus, "No one can do these signs that you do apart from the presence of God." (John 3.2)

What was Jesus' purpose? By what authority was Jesus doing these things? Did He have some new truth to reveal? In the atmosphere of curiosity that surrounded Him, Jesus got directly to the heart of the matter, "Very truly I tell you, no one can see the kingdom of God without being born from above." (John 3.3)

Jesus used a basic earthly category – human birth – to illuminate a profound spiritual reality. The phrase "born from above" or "born again" is arresting and fresh, alive with meaning. It points to another chance, starting over, and a new life!

In our current age, we toss these phrases about as if they were simply another fad, a chic "in" phrase, or just more "religious" talk. Even in church circles, sad to say, these phrases have become shopworn and jaded, part of our professional jargon, sapped of their original radical meaning. This new birth to which Jesus referred is a new beginning, a starting over again. This is a new life given by God Himself, a breaking into the world of His grace, a supernatural act bringing forth a new creation. God gives Himself to a particular person, who in receiving Him is born anew. This newborn person can now understand a new order of being, the kingdom of God. One is given new eyes and a new heart; a child of God living in joyful obedience to the Father's will.

Can this new birth happen today in you and me? A neighbor of mine is certain that it can. He told me recently, along with his wife, about being invited to a gospel concert. This certainly wasn't his thing, but knowing that his wife wanted to go he gave in and joined the group. During the concert, he heard the tenor sing "Only Jesus Knows." That song touched him where he was. In my neighbor's words, "Only Jesus knew what I was feeling and crying about many times in my life." The concert was the turning point in his life, and the Lord began to change him. "God took away my habit of drinking alcohol, a problem I have had since the age of 14," my neighbor explained. This gentleman was born again and he knew it.

So it is with each of us! The claim of Jesus comes to each of us this way – personally and directly to the very center of our existence. Birth from above cannot be manipulated or programmed. It is a gift given in God's own way and time – unseen but real. This breath of God brings life. God loves us and directs that love toward us with the intent that none of us remain untouched and unchanged. Why not let God take a hold of your life?

A WAKE-UP CALL
REFLECTION/QUEST TIME

• EXPLORING QUESTIONS FOR DISCUSSION
1. Are you willing to let God birth you anew, at whatever cost?
2. Can you think of an event or moment in your life when you have felt God acting in His own way in your life to lead you to a new birth?

• RELATED SCRIPTURE SOURCES
John 3:1-21   Colossians 3:10-17

2 Corinthians 5:17-21   Revelation 21:5-8

• NEW PERSPECTIVES
Consider personal changes you can make and/or new steps you can take to be of service to others.

• QUESTIONS TO BE RESOLVED
(Can be listed on a separate page)

• A PRAYER THOUGHT

"God, who commanded the light to shine out of darkness, has shined in our hearts, to give us knowledge of the glory of God in the face of Jesus Christ."

"May we all, beholding as in a glass the glory of the Lord, be changed into the same image from glory to glory, even as by the Spirit of the Lord."

THE RISK OF FALLING INTO
THE GRASP OF THE LIVING GOD

There are moments in everyone's life when we experience some sense of awe and wonder. Can you name these moments special to you? These moments of surprise and inspiration arrive in our lives as serendipity. Let's list a few possibilities: perhaps the birth of a child, the view of a beautiful sunrise, or the arrival of a splendorous sunset. Great moments in music or entering a cathedral to worship can also be memorable experiences. A kindly word of encouragement or a whispered "thank you" from an unexpected source can make a lasting impression on the heart.

For me, a visit to the Grand Canyon and the mule trip down the hairpin trail along the precipice of the canyon walls was a defining moment. Given that a slip could have been a quarter of a mile straight down, inspired in me a flush of fear . . . mixed with wonder. John Alexander, a traveler down the canyon, compares the mule ride with the fear of God. "The Grand Canyon is not designed for ease of human use but as a display of the grandeur of God and God's creation. It is the kind of spectacle that should strike us dumb and give us a sense of our smallness and creatureliness. The kind of place that can return us to reality after the shallow existence we accept as normal living . . . The kind of place where you can easily experience joy and peace – and easily get killed."

This leads us to a portion of Scripture that features Isaiah, a college-age youth who entered the Temple in Jerusalem to pray. (Isaiah 6:1-8) While at worship in the Temple, young Isaiah is given a stunning vision of God and receives his call to be a prophet. It is portrayed as if the windows of Heaven opened. "I saw the Lord!" Isaiah exclaims. The heavenly choir shouts, "Holy, holy, holy is the Lord of hosts; the whole earth is full of His glory."

To worship in church, the synagogue, or a mosque is to risk falling into the grasp of the living God. There are moments when we can share in Isaiah's experience of awe and unworthiness. To stand in the presence of God is as it was with Isaiah, to be brought to your knees. "Holy, holy, holy" is followed by "Woe is me! I am lost, for I am a man of unclean lips . . . my eyes have seen the King, the Lord of hosts!" (Isaiah 6:5)

Our pretensions become as nothing, and we recoil from the gaze of the one who is so good, so just, so holy that we fall to our knees and say as did Peter when he was face to face with the godliness of Jesus, "Go away from me Lord, for I am a sinful man!" (Luke 5:8) Unclean lips. Sin. Theologian William Willimon suggests that the sin being confessed here has not to do with some obvious misstep in our conduct or attitude, but rather the gaping chasm between who we are and who God is. Our real uncleanness is not just a sin of hurting someone or a troublesome neglect, but the gap between ourselves and God.

God's holiness is the mirror through which our pretentious goodness is seen for what it really is. Any of us, by a little Sunday jaunt into church, a little listening to a little sermon, a little anthem by a pretty little choir, can catch a glimpse of God and get more than we expected. We are left to cry like Isaiah, "Woe is me! I am lost. I am of unclean lips. Go away from me." But God never does. Across the gap between God and us, He reaches in love. He touches our lips. He calls us to Him. We are changed. We have fallen into hands of the living God.

THE RISK OF FALLING INTO THE GRASP OF THE LIVING GOD

REFLECTION/QUEST TIME

• EXPLORING QUESTIONS FOR DISCUSSION

1. Can you recall having experienced a stunning vision of God providing surprise and inspiration? What were the circumstances?

2. Like Isaiah, have you ever sensed a call to serve God in a particular way? Were you struck by a sense of awe and/or unworthiness?

3. Does the recognition of God's holiness create a gap between yourself and God? How might you best negotiate it?

• RELATED SCRIPTURE SOURCES

Isaiah 6:1-8   Romans 14:17-19

Isaiah 6:5   Luke 5:8

• NEW PERSPECTIVES

Consider personal changes you can make and/or new steps you can take to be of service to others.

• QUESTIONS TO BE RESOLVED

(Can be listed on a separate page)

• A PRAYER THOUGHT

"Take time to be holy, speak oft with thy Lord;
Abide with Him always, and feed on His Word."

Making Something Beautiful Out of Our Brokenness

"Have a good day" has become a rather common complimentary closing offered by restaurant cashiers, store clerks or just a farewell from a good friend. It leaves an atmosphere of pleasant sentiments and a sense of best wishes.

A few years ago, while spending a couple of days in the Poconos at our favorite retreat spot, Spruce Lake Retreat, I was doing some stargazing when I saw in the nearby cluster of trees a glowing campfire and heard some exuberant voices singing camp songs. It drew me like a magnet to come close and take in the festive event.

The flickering flames of light burned off sparkling reflections of what I came to realize were chrome handles and the frameworks of a large circle of wheelchairs, crutches, and braces that were supporting handicapped youths and adults. I began to realize that this was the closing assembly of a camping conference for people with handicaps. The leader was sitting in a wheelchair as she addressed the group and I heard her talk about something beautiful, something good.

Then she sang a solo and invited the whole gang to join her. The words were piercing. They moved deeply within and have been embedded ever since: "Something beautiful, something good. All my confusion He understood. All I had to offer Him was brokenness and strife. But He made something beautiful of my life." I sing these words and their accompanying melody regularly.

Who among us has not experienced moments or months of confusion? Who among us is without some level of brokenness? That circle of people with visible handicaps has touched me for a lifetime. They had a melody and a message. They passed on something beautiful, something good.

A few weeks ago, I heard something of this same theme of brokenness in the comments of a previous student who graduated from Moravian Theological Seminary. He was Douglas Kleintop who was elected as a new bishop of the Moravian Church at the Provincial Synod.

When asked for comments following his election, Doug began by showing a meaningful piece of broken glass given to him by the late Bishop James Weingarth, who was known for his presentation and distribution of broken glass which was collected on the beaches of the Atlantic Coast. Rather than collecting beautiful shells, the bishop collected broken glass smoothed over by the sand and the currents of the seaside.

To youth at camp, seminarians, parishioners, and anyone who would listen, he spoke of pieces of glass being symbolic of our lives in our brokenness. He always followed through with the message and ministry of Jesus, who transformed broken lives with His healing touch for bodies and souls. Bishop-elect Kleintop finds great inspiration for the ministry of Christ and the Church in shepherding those who recognize their brokenness.

This is a message for our time, for our lives. Out of our brokenness and strife, Jesus can make something beautiful, something good of our lives. This is that moment of transformation to get beyond those nagging, mental, emotional and/or spiritual handicaps which mar our wholeness. Why not let go and let God do it?

MAKING SOMETHING BEAUTIFUL
OUT OF OUR BROKENNESS
REFLECTION/QUEST TIME

• EXPLORING QUESTIONS FOR DISCUSSION
1. Do you recognize any evidence of brokenness in your life? How would you describe it – in writing or in another form of artistic expression?
2. What did Jesus promise to those who were broken in body and spirit?
3. Do you believe that God can transform you? What role will you play in this transformation?

• RELATED SCRIPTURE SOURCES

Romans 12:1-3   Jeremiah 23:9-10
Psalm 147:2-6   2 Corinthians 3:17-18
Acts 11:13-18

• NEW PERSPECTIVES
Consider personal changes you can make and/or new steps you can take to be of service to others.

• QUESTIONS TO BE RESOLVED
(Can be listed on a separate page)

• A PRAYER THOUGHT

"Spirit of the living God, fall afresh on me;
Spirit of the living God, fall afresh on me.
Melt me, mold me, fill me, use me.
Spirit of the living God, fall afresh on me."

TEXT AND TUNE: Daniel Iverson©1963 by Birdwing Music
(a div. of The Sparrow Corp.). All rights administered by the Sparrow Corp.
All rights reserved. Used by permission.

What Will I See If I Drive to the Top of the World?

Have you ever dreamed of what would be for you an ideal vacation? Have you ever wondered like an inquisitive explorer, "What will I see if I drive to the top of the world?" This question captures what my wife and I experienced one summer when our sons gave us an unexpected vacation for our 50th Wedding Anniversary. We enjoyed a two-week Alaska Cruise and Adventure Ashore in the heartland of Alaska.

Traveling into the interior of Alaska by way of a sternwheeler riverboat introduced us to delightful features of Alaskan culture. We were introduced to the late Susan Butcher, Iditorad Champion and Alaskan legend, as she described dog-mushing, visions of life on the trail, packing freight, feeding dogs, sleeping in the snow, and engaging in the Arctic challenge.

Such is the stuff of which legends are made. Susan was just such a legend. Our boat stopped at her home for a visit where she talked to our group and demonstrated her dog team's skills. Susan led the only climbing party to conquer the highest point on the North American continent by dog team, when she mushed to the top of 20,320 foot Mount McKinley.

During our land tours, we traveled on a scenic motorcoach journey to Denali National Park and Preserve on a natural history tour. We reached the wilderness to observe the wildlife in one of our country's most treasured public lands. We saw a living tapestry. Tundra carpeted with tiny wildflowers, and braided rivers from the action of freezing and thawing. Their banks embroidered with the tracks of sheep and caribou. Nature's loom never rests.

Denali is a national treasure, in part, because it is a place where visitors may still see large animals at home in the wild: caribou, bear, wolf, Dall sheep and moose. This preserve remains a stronghold not only for individual species but also for patterns of relationships. These relationships form the loom upon which true wilderness is woven: water, soil, rock, and air; fungi, plants, and animals both big and small; the seen and the unseen. In the continued weaving of its wilderness, Denali is a living masterpiece.

What will I see if I drive to the top of the world? The snow-capped glaciers provide a spectacular image of lofty mountain ranges, shrouded frequently by clouds which also enclose misty bays, enhancing the deep emerald green of the forests and meadows. There is a romantic touch to it all. Awe emerges in every moment. As we stand in silent fixation over the hills and are reminded of the psalmist's plaintive call to "be still and know that I am God" (Psalm 46:10), we are exhorted to marvel not only at the vaulted creation but also to envision the power of the Creator.

The psalmist, nestled in the hills of Israel, marveled in their glory and exclaimed, "I lift up my eyes to the hills – from where will my help come? My help comes from the Lord, who made heaven and earth. He will not let your foot be moved; He who keeps you will not slumber." (Psalm 121:1-3) God made not only the hills but heaven and earth as well. We should never trust in lesser power than God Himself. We never outgrow our need for God's untiring watch over our lives.

Beyond the excitement and grandeur of scenic Alaska is to know that the Great Creator deserves to be our Savior and all God's beauty can dwell within our lives. And each of us must ask, is God's handiwork evident in the living of our days? A little chorus sums up the quest:

> Let the beauty of Jesus be seen in me
> All His wonderful passion and purity
> O Thou Spirit divine, all my nature refine
> Till the beauty of Jesus be seen in me.

WHAT WILL I SEE IF I DRIVE TO THE TOP OF THE WORLD?

• **EXPLORING QUESTIONS FOR DISCUSSION**
1. Can you think of moments, when in awe, you have been struck by the grandeur of God? What were the circumstances? How did it change your thinking or appreciations? Might this become a worship experience similar to Psalm 33?
2. What would be your ideal vacation? Why? Are there particular ingredients you desire or need in a vacation?
3. Can the beauty and strength of Jesus be seen in you?

• **RELATED SCRIPTURE SOURCES**
>Psalm 4:10   Psalm 121:1-4
>Psalm 33:1-22

• **NEW PERSPECTIVES**
Consider personal changes you can make and/or new steps you can take to be of service to others.

• **QUESTIONS TO BE RESOLVED**
(Can be listed on a separate page)

• **A PRAYER THOUGHT**

"We thank You for the season of the spirit, for joy and sorrow, for pleasure and pain, for gladness and grief, for friendship and solitude.

We are grateful to You for your sustaining presence in all circumstances, and for giving us the strength through which we can do all things.

We pray for those who because of greed or selfishness exploit the gifts of the earth, that they may learn to be careful stewards of Your creation.

We pray for all who by their commitment and involvement are working to preserve our planet, that You would multiply their efforts.

We pray for those who suffer from prejudice, poverty, or pain, that You would draw near to them and provide for them true justice and mercy."

CHAPTER II

GOD'S LOVE
Promises

What does God promise to people of faith? The symbol above portrays the dove, found in the story of Noah, with a freshly plucked olive leaf in his beak evidencing dry ground and a new beginning. This represents the origin of God's covenant for all generations to come. And the rainbow, we are told, will be a sign of God's remembrance of His everlasting covenant with His creation.

The New Testament reveals God's new covenant with His creation. Jesus points to the promise of God in Luke 24:49 (KJV), stating, "Behold, I send forth the promise of My Father upon you." In 1 John 2:25, this promise is identified as "eternal life." It is planted by God in this life, and finds fruition beyond death in the full presence of Him.

Does the Joy of Living Inspire Progress?

School days begin each year as summer ends and the fall season opens its gates to learning. The story is told of a young boy, whose excitement for sports outdistanced his devotion to studies. When report cards were given out, he put off showing his to his parents as long as he could. Finally the moment of truth could be avoided no longer. His parents read the grades with concern but no surprise. Then they read his teacher's comments in the report: "Johnny does well at school, but he could do much better if the sheer joy of living didn't impede his progress."

One can picture Johnny in the classroom, wriggling about and waiting anxiously for recess or the school day to end so he could play. At this stage of his life, being a pitcher was more important than algebra or the facts of history. Each of us can relate to Johnny's story; as children, each of us eagerly sought to just play! In fact, we know at heart that the teacher's analysis of Johnny's predicament was not true! The joy of living never impeded anyone's progress. It inspires it! We all long to experience the sheer joy of living.

So does Jesus. And He tells us how. Luke 14:25-35 is a compilation of several of His parables that describe the nature, conditions, and resources for abundant living. The parables in this passage all lead up to the climax in verses 34 and 35: "Salt is good; but if salt has lost its taste, how can its saltiness be restored? It is fit neither for the soil nor for the manure pile; they throw it away. Let anyone with ears to hear listen!"

Jesus came to provide His followers with a tangy approach to living: distinctive, sharp and pungent. Salty people with an incisive quality that seasons the life of others and society bring zest and gusto to life. Like salt, one can bring out the best of the flavor of living.

Jesus calls His followers to be like salt. Salt has two properties: it flavors life and it preserves it from corruption. When you and I live without excuses as those loved and forgiven, we flavor life everywhere – at the office, at home, and in our place of worship. We become the preserving element – those who stand for justice and righteousness despite the world's corruption.

We've all heard the phrase, "Today is the first day of the rest of your life." The reverse is also true, "Today can be the last day of your past." Today can be the day when we resolve, with God's help, to live this next day and the remaining years of our life making no excuses. Life is now in session. Are we willing to be the salty tang which brings flavor to the world, to your neighborhood, to our home?

DOES THE JOY OF LIVING INSPIRE PROGRESS?
REFLECTION/QUEST TIME

- **EXPLORING QUESTIONS FOR DISCUSSION**
1. Many Christians blend into the world and avoid the cost of standing up for Christ. Jesus taught that if believers lose their distinctive saltiness they become worthless. How salty are you?
2. Where do you help to season your surroundings?
3. Can you cite some examples where you are or should be preserving the good in your community and bringing new flavor to life?
4. What are the costs of being a disciple, which often tempts us to turn back from our commitments?

- **RELATED SCRIPTURE SOURCES**
  Luke 14:25-35   Philippians 3:7-16
  Hebrews 11:23-28

- **NEW PERSPECTIVES**
Consider personal changes you can make and/or new steps you can take to be of service to others.

- **QUESTIONS TO BE RESOLVED**
(Can be listed on a separate page)

- **A PRAYER THOUGHT**

"Teach me Thy patience, still with Thee in clearer, dearer company. In work that keeps faith sweet and strong, in trust that triumphs over wrong."

WHAT IS THE DRIVING FORCE IN YOUR LIFE?

Most of us have a startling awareness that we are living in changing times. America and Americans are sizably different than just 10 years ago. We have been inundated by a tremendous volume of changes. Some changes appear to be for the good. Others appear to have catastrophic consequences for the future.

Have you ever been aware of a time or times when your life has collided with your beliefs? Change contributes to such collisions, sometimes leading to economic, domestic, vocational or moral shipwrecks. How have you resolved collisions of your values or beliefs with life's changes?

One of my youthful experiences came with my first job offer. I had just turned sixteen years of age and received my driver's license, when I responded to an ad in the newspaper for a part-time job driving a delivery truck for a hotel and bar supply company. I was offered the job and accepted it. I couldn't wait to announce my joy to the family at the supper table that evening. To my surprise, my father responded to my announcement with a rather firm declaration that I couldn't accept my first job offer and make use of my new driver's license. He instructed me to call the employer and inform him that I couldn't accept his offer. My father added his reasoning. He did not want me to be exposed to the atmosphere or influence of bar rooms. If I wanted a job, he would hire me to work in his construction business.

I was crestfallen. But with maturity and my father's thoughtful guidance, I came to appreciate his wisdom. As an adolescent, the driving force in my life was the lure of the immediate. My father's focus was living a purpose for the long haul. He was in tune with the understanding of Isaiah, the Old Testament prophet, who commented, "Those of steadfast mind you keep in peace – in peace because they trust in You." (Isaiah 26:3)

What drives your life? Everyone's life is driven by something. Whether we are driving a car, a nail, or a golf ball, we are guiding, controlling, and directing it at that moment. Many people are driven by guilt, resentment and anger, materialism, or the expectations of others. Author Rick Warren in his book, *The Purpose Driven Life*, states, "Nothing matters more than knowing God's purposes for our life. We are all products of our past but we don't have to be prisoners of it. God's purpose is not limited by our past . . . He can do amazing things with the rest of our lives."

There is more to life than just here and now. We are made to last forever. Scripture reminds us that "the world and its desire are passing away, but those who do the will of God live forever." (1 John 2:17) God has designed us in His image to live for eternity. The reason we feel we should live forever is because God wired our brains with that desire! God has planted eternity in the human heart. (Ecclesiastes 3:11) As St. Paul explains in his letter to the believers in Corinth, we must not focus on "what can be seen but [on] what cannot be seen; for what can be seen is temporary, but what cannot be seen is eternal." (2 Corinthians 4:18)

WHAT IS THE DRIVING FORCE IN YOUR LIFE?
REFLECTION/QUEST TIME

• **EXPLORING QUESTIONS FOR DISCUSSION**
1. Have there been times in your life when life circumstances have collided with your beliefs and/or values?
2. What is driving your life now? Are there some changes which you ought to be making? List them.
3. Consider what you might ask of God in prayer in order to make these changes possible.

• **RELATED SCRIPTURE SOURCES**
    Isaiah 26:3   1 John 2:17
    Ecclesiastes 3:11

• **NEW PERSPECTIVES**
Consider personal changes you can make and/or new steps you can take to be of service to others.

• **QUESTIONS TO BE RESOLVED**
(Can be listed on a separate page)

• **A PRAYER THOUGHT**

"Come now, Oh Lord, and search each inmost thought.
Ask if we love and serve Thee as we ought.
Do we attempt to do Thy Holy Will?
Does constant love for this our bosoms fill?"

Spirituality – What Is It?

Have you ever heard someone say about another person, "He is so heavenly-minded that he is no earthly good"? I haven't heard this comment in recent years. Perhaps this is because the high rise of secularism and materialism throughout our society has permeated so thoroughly that the religious and non-religious alike have become more earthly-minded to the neglect of the spiritual.

Auto racing has emerged as the largest spectator sport in America. I live close to a nearby raceway, so I often hear the deep roar of the racing engines and see the thousands of fans make their way to this automotive attraction. Undoubtedly, racing has a magnetic thrill and romance for many, despite the preponderance of noise, the abundance of exhaust fumes, and the endless circles in hours around a track. Circular high speed racing may be a parable of our times. Talking about spirituality or a spiritual journey with such a backdrop may seem strangely out of place.

Spirituality – what is it? By its very nature spirituality involves biblical, theological, historical, and personal perspectives. One of the most difficult aspects of discussing spiritual growth is trying to discern just what it is that one is talking about. One person says, "My spiritual life constitutes my relationships with other people." Another says, "Spirituality for me is worshipping, reading the Bible and praying." Still another says, "Spirituality is coming into harmony with God, true liberation and salvation." And then someone says, "It seems to me that all life is spiritual. There is nothing that is not spiritual about life."

Each statement is touching on something of the truth. Words, alone, cannot do justice to what is being described. There is no way to choose words which everyone will find acceptable. Furthermore, there simply are no words to describe the deepest levels of human spiritual experience. All spirituality is a response to God's call. We can only hope to identify the nature of the spiritual pilgrimage, and the experimental disciplines and practices which undergird discipleship.

We are all engaged in making a journey of our soul. On this journey which involves tumult, strain, conflict and anxiety, we need to reach the conviction that God is ALL. All takes place within His grasp. God alone matters, God alone is. Our spiritual life is God's affair. It consists of being drawn, at His pace and in His way, to the place He wants us to be, not to the place that we fancy. Much of our life is used up craving to and fussing about the material, political, social, emotional, intellectual, and even the religious plane. Some new development is needed for us to abandon the three verbs: to Want, to Have, to Do. They are transcended by, and included in, the fundamental verb: to Be. Being not wanting, having or doing is the essence of spiritual life. Spiritual formation deals with one's relationship with God and the individual's attainment of a larger ability to understand and respond to God's unique call to him or her.

A God-seeker is a person on a journey. But an authentic spirituality suggests that we become more than wanderers meandering aimlessly in all directions. The Psalmist describes it well when writing about his relationship with God, "O Lord, you have searched me and known me. You know when I sit down and when I rise up; You discern my thoughts from far away. You search out my path and my lying down, and are acquainted with all my ways." (Psalm 139:2-3)

It is not a journey alone. St. Paul wrote to the fledgling community of Christians in the city of Colossae, "As you therefore have received Christ Jesus the Lord, continue to live your lives in Him, rooted and built up in Him and established in the faith, just as you were taught, abounding in thanksgiving." (Colossians 2:6-7) In this recognition the journey in faith begins. It is a story of new beginnings. We become members of a community struggling to live in the world in a new way. It is worth the risk to let ourselves be formed and empowered by the person of Jesus Christ.

Spirituality – What Is It?
Reflection/Quest Time

• Exploring Questions for Discussion

1. How would you define "spirituality?" How have you expressed your spirituality?

2. Describe your adventures into the spiritual. Are you a wanderer or a journeyer?

3. Has God called to you? What does He expect of you?

• Related Scripture Sources

Psalm 139:2   Colossians 2:6-8

• New Perspectives

Consider personal changes you can make and/or new steps you can take to be of service to others.

• Questions to be Resolved

(Can be listed on a separate page)

• A Prayer Thought

"Gracious God, for revealing Yourself to us and who created all things, who gave us dominion over all the earth, who called us into a covenant relationship with You, who has given us the power of being Your ambassador in our world, who loves us as Your children through Jesus Christ our Lord, we give You our heartfelt thanks."

Carelessness in Pie Making and Personal Lifestyle Can Result in Tragedy and Pain

If all of us sat together in a circle and began recounting some of our most embarrassing moments, we would probably be engrossed in unending laughter for hours at a time. What would be one of your most embarrassing moments?

For me, I recall an early pastoral experience when one of the high school youth groups of the parish was sponsoring a bake sale at a local market in order to raise money to go to summer church camp. I wanted to do my part, so I volunteered to supply a homemade pie. My hope was that the real pie maker in our family, my wife, would do the honors. As luck would have it, when Saturday morning rolled around, my wife was not feeling well and was unable to assemble and bake a pie. She assured me that pie making was just a matter of following the directions on the box, and suggested with confidence in my abilities that I could bake the pie myself. I asked her what would be the easiest pie to make, and she suggested a lemon meringue pie because we had the ingredients.

Time for the bake sale seemed to rush into the kitchen like a fast moving train, and I began my mixing and measuring in haste while the oven heated up. I kept returning to my wife's bedside to get more accurate interpretations of the process, and she kept encouraging me in my efforts. Soon the ingredients went into the oven, and before long I removed the pie, wrapped it in silver paper, put it on the floor of our Volkswagen, and proudly rushed my prize creation to the youth and their advisor at the bake sale.

A couple of times on the way to the market, I had to make a few quick stops at red lights, not realizing what that could do to the pie. As I lifted the pie out of the car, I noticed some yellow ingredients on the floor mat and discovered that my pie was more of a yellow goo than a picturesque lemon meringue pie that I had envisioned. Apparently in my wish to meet the deadline, I did not give the pie time to cool down and jell.

With a red face and sizeable frustration, I handed the covered goo to the advisor and advised her to notify the youth that the pie had arrived and was already sold. I bought it, but asked her to put it under the table for me to pick up when I returned at the end of the day. I returned later in the afternoon and she said her dog had eaten the pie. That event ended my pie making career and the dog survived.

I've learned that there are some basic principles in pie making that one simply cannot neglect or rush. To avoid these essential practices only invites embarrassment and pain.

Life and faith are like that also. Personal lifestyle and national carelessness can lead to a slippery slope. We are living in a time when little news is good news. National polls suggest massive evidence of rising pessimism in the direction our country seems to be heading. Sizeable chunks of our personal lives and national trends are the source of decay. The fear and embarrassment is real.

History has something to say to us. Edward Gibbon in his *Decline and Fall of the Roman Empire* suggests the following as the five major reasons for the collapse of the Roman Empire: 1) Family life had disintegrated; 2) Traditional ethical systems were ignored and discarded; "anything goes" had become the prevailing attitude of the day; 3) Entertainment had become perverse and immoral; 4) Vast amounts of money were being spent on maintaining the military machine in order to defend the Empire; and 5) The Empire's economy had collapsed. Surely, this leads us to wonder, "Is this history . . . or is it prophecy?" Perhaps it's both.

Present history points powerfully to the subtle strategies of the demonic that gather Americans around a banner that boasts, "Blessed! Rich! Successful! Superpower!" Perhaps this is the time to change one word in the song "God Bless America." Should we not be singing, "God Save America?"

In a personal way, the plea might better be "God save me." In the Gospel of John 7:7, Jesus points out that the world hates Him because He testifies that its works are evil. Note please! The created world is not evil – but the words and attitudes of the fallen humanity living in it are, and they continue to produce a tragic ripple effect. This is more than just an embarrassing moment. There are good reasons to believe that history is leading us in a direction that will force us to take corrective measures, rather than endlessly pleasuring ourselves with what we consider to be our rights and delights.

Is there a better time for us to stop, look, and listen, and take the passion of Christ seriously by taking up our cross and following Him? Perhaps we should be inspired by the example of St. Paul, who intoned his longing as follows: "I want to know Christ and the power of His resurrection and the sharing of His suffering by becoming like Him in His death, if somehow I may attain the resurrection from the dead." (Philippians 3:10-11)

CARELESSNESS IN PIE MAKING AND PERSONAL LIFESTYLE CAN RESULT IN TRAGEDY AND PAIN

REFLECTION/QUEST TIME

• EXPLORING QUESTIONS FOR DISCUSSION
1. Can you think of a time when you neglected the "right" way and the results were disastrous? What did you learn from this experience?
2. What do current trends in society lead us to believe about our lifestyles?
3. What does Jesus teach us?

• RELATED SCRIPTURE SOURCES
John 7:7   Philippians 3:10-14
Hebrews 12:1-2   Philippians 4:4-9, 13
Hebrews 2:9

• NEW PERSPECTIVES
Consider personal changes you can make and/or new steps you can take to be of service to others.

• QUESTIONS TO BE RESOLVED
(Can be listed on a separate page)

• A PRAYER THOUGHT

"We confess, Lord, that as Your disciples we have often dishonored the holy name we hear. We ask Your forgiveness for the times when we have failed to labor for Your kingdom; when we have not followed Your admonition to seek first the kingdom of God; when we have hidden our light from the world; when we, as the salt of the earth, have lost our strength. Have mercy on us, and restore unto us the joy of faithful discipleship.

The Lord, your Redeemer, has said: With everlasting love, I will have compassion on you. Therefore serve the Lord with gladness; witness to His goodness and mercy; and preach Jesus Christ as Lord, with yourselves as servants for Jesus' sake."

Does a Constant Search for Pleasure, Security, Ease and Comfort Make Life Worthwhile?

Mr. Newt Gingrich in setting forth ideas for the 1996 presidential campaign said, "I do not believe that any civilization can survive with 12-year-olds having babies, 15-year-olds killing each other, 17-year-olds dying of AIDS and 18-year-olds getting diplomas they can't even read." What an indictment of a people who are losing their way. What a wake-up call to our nation, which has been experiencing the zenith of our wealth and power as well as our worldwide influence. Is it possible that we are losing our soul? Did Jesus touch on this reality when He asked His disciple, "For what will it profit them to gain the whole world and forfeit their life?" (Mark 8:36)

In our day and generation, we seem to have met life with a constant search for pleasure, security, ease and comfort, and finding that we are losing all that makes life worthwhile. Life becomes a soft and flabby thing. Life becomes a selfish thing. Life becomes an earthbound thing. And in the process, we can discover that life is not worth living. What can we give, or do, or be to get life back again?

We would do well to recognize that in every decision of life we are doing something to ourselves. We are making a certain kind of person. We are building up steadily and inevitably a certain kind of self and character – and a certain kind of nation. It is perfectly possible for a person or nation to gain all things we set our hearts upon, and then to awaken one morning to find we have missed the most important things of all. To gain the world stands for all the material things, the excessive pleasurable pursuits, and the status symbols such as education and prestige as opposed to gaining a relationship with God.

The story is told of a little girl who lived with her grandmother after her parents died, and she slept in an upstairs bedroom. One night, there was a fire in the house and the grandmother perished while trying to rescue the child. The fire spread quickly, and the first floor of the house was soon engulfed in flames. Neighbors called the fire department, then stood helplessly by, unable to enter the house because flames blocked all entrances. The little girl appeared at an upstairs window, crying for help, just as word spread among the crowd that firefighters would be delayed a few minutes because they were all at another fire. Suddenly, a man appeared with a ladder, put it up against the side of the house and disappeared inside. When he reappeared, he had the little girl in his arms. He delivered the child to the waiting arms below and, then, disappeared into the night.

An investigation revealed that the child had no living relatives, and weeks later a meeting was held in the town hall to determine who would take the child into their home and bring her up. A teacher said she would like to raise the child. She pointed out that she could ensure a good education. A farmer offered her an upbringing on his farm. He pointed out that living on a farm was healthy and satisfying. Others spoke, giving their reasons why it was to the child's advantage to live with them. Finally, the town's richest resident arose and said, "I can give this child all the advantages that you have mentioned here, plus money and everything that money can buy."

Throughout all this, the child remained silent, her eyes focused on the floor. "Does anyone else want to speak?" asked the meeting chairman. A man came forward from the back of the hall. His gait was slow and he seemed in pain. When he got to the front of the room, he stood directly before the little girl and held out his arms. The crowd gasped. His hand and arms were terribly scarred. The child cried out, "This is the man who rescued me!" With a leap, she threw her arms around the man's neck, holding on for dear life, just as she had that fateful night. She buried her face in his shoulder and sobbed for a few minutes. Then she looked up and smiled at him.

"This meeting is adjourned," said the chairman.

The great challenge Jesus set forth to his disciples is ours' as well: "If any want to become My followers, let them deny themselves and take up their cross and follow Me. For those who want to save their life will lose it, and those who lose their life for My sake will find it. For what will it profit them if they gain the whole world but forfeit their life? Or what will they give in return for their life?" (Matthew 16.24-26)

Does a Constant Search for Pleasure, Security, Ease and Comfort Make Life Worthwhile?

Reflection/Quest Time

• **Exploring Questions for Discussion**

1. To gain the world includes the excessive accumulation of material things, the pursuit of pleasure, and the focus on achieving social prestige as opposed to seeking God's favor. Can the pursuit of these so-called assets cause you to lose your way?

2. What can we give, do, or be to get our relationship with God back on track?

3. Do you think that our society has lost its soul? Why or why not?

• **Related Scripture Sources**

Matthew 16:24-28   Psalm 72:13
James 1:21-27

• **New Perspectives**

Consider personal changes you can make and/or new steps you can take to be of service to others.

• **Questions to be Resolved**

(Can be listed on a separate page)

• **A Prayer Thought**

"Lord God, merciful and gracious, slow to anger, and abounding in steadfast love and faithfulness, keeping steadfast love for thousands, forgiving iniquity and transgression and sin; yet by means clearing the unrepentant. Incline Your ear and hear, for we do not present our supplications before You on the ground of our righteousness, but on the ground of Your great mercies."

"Create in us a clean heart, O God, and put a new and right spirit within us. Do not cast us away from Your presence and do not take Your Holy Spirit from us. Restore to us the joy of Your salvation, and sustain in us a willing spirit. Have mercy upon us according to Your steadfast love, according to Your abundant mercy, blot out our transgression through Jesus Christ our Savior."

CHOOSING TO BE FAITHFUL

The greatest power we possess is the power to choose. The weight of this truth came home to me recently at West Point Academy. It all happened during the Army-Lehigh football game, a lopsided contest won by Army. I was confronted with the dilemma of divided loyalties as a Bethlehem native and an Army veteran.

For whom should I cheer? I arrived on game day without benefit of knowing each team's skill and without reading some sportswriter's predictions. My quandary came primarily in the first quarter when the score was reasonably close. I found myself cheering for each team in their successes until the game tilted decidedly in Army's favor and I grew attached to the underdog. I became aware of my ambivalence when an unfamiliar couple next to me asked who I was rooting for. Their question forced me to make a choice.

As the Cadets rolled up the score, interest in the game waned and it was easy to be distracted. The pageantry surrounding an Army home game is unmatched, from a full-dress Cadet parade in the morning to resplendent skydivers descending with the game ball. Then there are the bands, bagpipers, cheerleaders, immaculate Army mules, and a cannon salute for each Army score. It's all witnessed from a perch majestically above the meandering Hudson River.

Whether it's a ballgame or the living of life, there are choices to be made. The power of choice is ultimately highlighted in consequences sure to follow. Moses in speaking to the Hebrew people, who were a small and insignificant group in powerful Egypt, encouraged them to "choose life," to love God and obey His commandments.

He was speaking to people who seemed not to have much of a chance. But Moses insisted that their existence and fortunes depended on their choice and their obedience to God's Word. He reminded them that God was showing His love for them as a people, and they in turn should choose to love God in the decisions they made.

A people of faith face the difficulty of being faithful in a culture losing its soul. All of us would do well to consider the following questions: "Just who are you rooting for?" "Do you know where you are headed?" "Do you realize what this means for now and the future?"

We are called to choose in the context of God's love – the one creative force. There are many attractions and a lot of sideshows that can distract us from the main event. The salient message is found in the message of Moses: love the Lord your God, obey Him, hold fast to Him. This means life.

Choosing To Be Faithful
Reflection/Quest Time

• Exploring Questions for Discussion

1. Regular self-examination is crucial as we face the constant battle between good and evil. Every decision we engage is loaded with consequences involving life and death. What have been some major decisions that you have made that have changed your life course – for better and for worse?

2. What does the declaration of Saint Paul mean to you when he says in Philippians 1:21, "For to me, living is Christ and dying is gain"?

3. We are called to choose, in the context of God's love, the one creative force. What does this mean for your future?

• Related Scripture Sources

Deuteronomy 30:11-20   John 15:1-25
Isaiah 7:15   Philippians 1:19-26

• New Perspectives

Consider personal changes you can make and/or new steps you can take to be of service to others.

• Questions to be Resolved

(Can be listed on a separate page)

• A Prayer Thought

"Most merciful God, we confess that we have sinned against You in thought, word, and deed, by what we have done, and by what we have left undone. We have not loved You with our whole heart; we have not loved our neighbors as ourselves. We are truly sorry, and we humbly repent. For the sake of your Son Jesus Christ, have mercy on us and forgive us, that we may delight in Your will, and walk in Your ways, to the glory of Your name. Amen."

"The Lord says: I, even I, am the God who blots out your transgressions for My own sake and will not remember your sins. Go and sin no more."

How Available is God To Our Prayers?

Have you ever wondered why we find so little time to pray? And when we take time, why is it often an unsatisfactory experience? Have you ever been frustrated by what seemed to be unanswered prayers? Are there times when you wonder why prayer appears to be a dynamic dialogue for some, while for you it is often a monotonous monologue, as if no one were listening? Does prayer change the course of events, or is it simply to change us to be able to live in what seems to be irrevocable and unchangeable?

We wonder about prayer. What is it, really? How can we pray effectively? Why do we resist its power?

We join the disciples in expressing our need: "Lord, teach us to pray!" The Lord's answer in Luke 11:1-13 was to give them a model prayer which we can call the Disciples' Prayer. He knew that the disciples' deepest question was not how to pray but, knowing as much as they did about the power of prayer, why they often didn't resort to prayer.

Picture a typical one-room Palestinian house. It is divided into two parts. The main floor is used for the family's life during the day, and the stable is used during the night. At one end is a loft where the family eats and sleeps. At sunset the cattle are brought in and the door is tightly bolted at the crossbar. Soon afterward, the whole family goes to sleep in the loft, the cattle settle down, and all is dark and quiet.

Then at midnight, when everyone is sleeping soundly, a persistent knock beats on the heavy wooden door. Who can that be at this hour of the night? An old friend has come to the village and has no place to stay. Hospitality demands that the friend be fed. The host is aghast to find he has no bread to express his welcome and care.

His neighbor will help! Or will he? His family also has bedded down for the night. The midnight knock shifts the scene to the neighbor whose voice is angry and perturbed: "Who's there? What do you want at this hour of the night?"

"Friend, lend me three loaves of bread, for a friend of mine has arrived, and I have nothing to set before him." (Luke 11:5-6) The whole family and the cattle are restless. The whole household is disrupted. The neighbor responds with the gift of needed bread.

Then, suddenly, Jesus is in serious conversation with us. He's drawn us into a comparison we didn't expect. If a man finally would respond because of the importunity of his neighbor, would not God, who "neither slumbers nor sleeps"

(See Psalm 121:3), answer our prayers? "Ask, and it will be given you; search, and you will find; knock, and the door will be opened for you." (Matthew 7:7)

What has God told us about Himself and how we can communicate with Him? God is one who listens and responds with a gift beyond our wildest expectations. Our deepest questions about prayer can be answered. God is not a reluctant neighbor. Jesus wants us to know the ready availability of God. God wants to give us a gift. More than answers to prayer, He wants to give us Himself. Mother Teresa of Calcutta put it clearly: "Prayer enlarges the heart until it is capable of containing God's gift of Himself."

How Available is God To Our Prayers?
Reflection/Quest Time

• **Exploring Questions for Discussion**

1. Hospitality is a central teaching of the Bible. Consider your level of hospitality towards the following:

Strangers	The poor
Other races	The wealthy
Religious people	The young
Non-religious people	The old

2. What factors influence your level of hospitality?

3. How would you describe your prayer life, and the balance of answered and unanswered prayers?

• **Related Scripture Sources**

Luke 11:1-13   Luke 11:5-6
Psalm 121:3, 9, 10

• **New Perspectives**

Consider personal changes you can make and/or new steps you can take to be of service to others.

• **Questions to be Resolved**

(Can be listed on a separate page)

• **A Prayer Thought**

"In the awareness that we are one with all human creation, we pray about the issues that confront us all.

For our planet and the environment in which we live,
For the end of war, ethnic conflict, and all violence,
For liberation from racism, bigotry, and injustice,
For freedom from addictions of all kinds,
For the end of abuse of children, women, and men,
For each member of the human family, that all may know the dignity
        and worth of being a child of God,
For solutions to our common human dilemmas, and for our dedication
        to be part of those solutions."

SEEING THE WORLD
FROM GOD'S PERSPECTIVE

Most of us have gone through some form of reality testing. From our earliest childhood days, we have created and lived-out homemade fantasies. For periods of time and play, we lived in worlds built by our own imaginations. Our toys and random objects around us took on projections which in our dream world became larger than life. And then as we grew older, in small as well as sudden ways, our fantasies gave way to new realities. We began to wonder: What are things made of? What is ultimate? What is it that everything depends on for its existence? What is really real? Many philosophers have found it necessary to conceive of reality in two spheres or levels: what appears to be real and what is real.

In earlier years, my 15-year-old grandson invited me to take him on a motor tour of different used car dealers so as to look at available Jeeps for sale. While it was a year before he could get a driver's license and even longer to be able to purchase a Jeep on his own, I considered it a rare privilege to join my imaginative grandson in one of his choice dreams and preoccupations. I remember my own interests in cars at this early age. As we traveled to our first stop, I asked him what this Jeep he envisioned would look like. He described it quickly with at least five particular features.

To my surprise, our first visit to a car agency had one Jeep, and it had every feature my grandson was looking for! A friendly salesman quickly joined us in our review, even though I reminded him that we were only exploring and that I was an intermediary in the absence of this young man's father who would be making all decisions. We were given the privilege of driving the Jeep. It more than passed our every expectation. Upon a return from our test ride, a sales proposal with a very attractive price was drawn-up and given to our grandson. He was greatly honored. The salesman took him for real. He couldn't wait to present the purchase proposal to his father later that same night.

A full family review evolved, and it wasn't long before our phone rang and I was being asked about what I had done! Now, the time for reality testing was facing all of us. Grandfather, father, and son had to deal with some deep questions of responsibility and rightness in decision-making. Only the eventual sale of the Jeep to another customer saved the day – actually for another year, when time and maturity would provide added wisdom.

In speaking to the church in Corinth, St. Paul commented, "When I was a child, I spoke like a child, I thought like a child, I reasoned like a child; when I became an adult, I put an end to childish ways. For now we see in a mirror, dimly, but then we will see face to face. Now I know only in part; then I will know fully, even as I have been fully known." (1 Corinthians 13:11-12) Such mirrors as Paul had in mind were made of polished metals of silver and bronze. But at best they reflected no clear image. So it is with our comprehension of God. We have no clear image.

The reality and majesty of God is dimmed by the problem of physical evil. Wars, famine and death, human suffering, and natural catastrophes cast their shadows over the being of God. Man does not understand. We try to trust and believe that our lives are set in the midst of a friendly universe. But we see as in a mirror dimly.

Through the strange and varied pageant of human history man seeks God. When one thinks of the trials and sufferings of the innocent and the righteous, and of all that is involved in the problem of moral and spiritual evil, it is often difficult to believe in the power, presence, and the infinite love and grace of God. Job's great exclamation is pertinent. "Oh, that I knew where I might find Him." (Job 23:3)

Our faith has to be at its best when things are at their worst. We see as in a mirror dimly. A great faith has always had to carry a heavy load of doubt, uncertainty, and inconclusiveness. We are offered a glimpse into the future to give us hope that one day we will be complete when we see God face to face. This truth should strengthen our faith – we don't have all the answers now, but then we will. Someday we will see Christ in person and be able to see with God's perspective. And it will be worth it all.

Seeing the World From God's Perspective
Reflection/Quest Time

• Exploring Questions for Discussion

1. Has your faith perspective gone beyond your "childish ways"? What do you see when you view God through mature eyes of faith?

2. What has your faith enabled you to see?

3. Are there some new realities which have enriched your understandings in what is really real? Name and describe your new understandings.

• Related Scripture Sources

1 Corinthians 13:11-13   Mark 10:13-16
Romans 14:21-23   2 Corinthians 5:7-8
Job – Chapter 23

• New Perspectives

Consider personal changes you can make and/or new steps you can take to be of service to others.

• Questions to be Resolved

(Can be listed on a separate page)

• A Prayer Thought

"Almighty God, You have given us grace at this time to make our common intercession to You, and You have promised through Your beloved Son that where two or three are gathered together in His name You will be in the midst of them. Fulfill now, O Lord, our desires and petitions as may be best for us, granting us in this world knowledge of Your truth, and in the world to come life everlasting."

An Inward Look
at True Worship

Summer for many of us is vacation time. Vacation choices involve a host of activities, depending largely on what any one of us feel we desire or need at a given moment. Usually our purpose is to get away from our usual routine or site of operations to experience something new, something refreshing, as a means to get a new start on life. As a result, large segments of America take to the road or go on a flight or a cruise. Campsites are filled and beaches are crowded. Tourism is widespread.

Have you ever envisioned what would be the perfect vacation? Is there such a thing? This is an intriguing exercise and has about as many answers as there are people.

Our family, including grandparents, parents, and grandchildren, just returned from what we perceived to be a perfect vacation. We spent a week in the Adirondacks at a camp and conference center where they advertise "A Vacation with a Purpose." The center exists under spiritual motivations and has within its lakeside setting something for everyone, from the youngest to the oldest of family members. Among the many opportunities are swimming, boating, secular and sacred concerts, seminars, daily worship, crafts, group games and entertainment, or just plain relaxation. For our family all of these activities were sampled, as well as a day or two spent canoeing and whitewater rafting down the Scanadaga River.

For us, this Christian community of vacationers was, as St. Paul describes it in his letter to the church at Philippi, something of "a colony of heaven," where our kids could circulate freely without fear or uncertainty and the quality of atmosphere and activity ministered to the wholeness of our physical and spiritual well being. Upon our arrival home, there was a general consensus among us as a family that our lives have been shaped in new directions – physically, mentally, and spiritually. We truly experienced "a vacation with a purpose."

In speaking about true worship and essential change, Paul urges his readers to shape themselves according to their faith. One translation puts this portion of his letter to the believers in Rome like this, "Do not be conformed to this world, but be transformed by the renewing of your minds, so that you may discern what is the will of God – what is good and acceptable and perfect." (Romans 12:2) He further urges later in verse 21 of the same chapter not to be shaped by the reality of the world (evil) but to reshape the reality by the power of grace (good). Herein is a call for a radical change, where we are not conformed to the world but are transformed by it. How can this happen?

To explain how change can take place in our lives, the apostle Paul projects a concept of true worship. First, he suggests, we must present our bodies to God. He reminds us that our bodies belong to God and are a temple of the Holy Spirit. God lives in and works through individuals dedicated to Him. Our body is much like a church or cathedral. It is built for the offering of worship of the spirit of man to God. But it has to be designed by the mind of some architect; it has to be built by the hands of craftsmen and laborers; only then does it become a shrine when people meet to worship. It is most literally a product of the mind, the body, and the spirit of man. We are to take our body; take all the tasks and activities that we have to do every day; take the ordinary work of the shop, the office, the home, the shipyard, the mine, and our vacations; and offer all that as an act of worship to God. Real worship is the offering of everyday life to God, not just something which is transacted in a church or synagogue or mosque.

Worship involves a change of our inward personality – the very essence of our being in a Christ-centered life. This happens, according to Paul, by the renewal of our minds. He goes on to indicate that when Christ comes into a person's life it results in a new person; the center of one's being is different; the mind becomes different. When Christ becomes the center of life then we can offer real worship, which is the offering of every moment and every action of life to God. Best of all this renewal and new creation can begin with "a vacation with a purpose." Try it! You will like it!

An Inward Look at True Worship
Reflection/Quest Time

- **Exploring Questions for Discussion**
1. What minor changes can you make in your life to live life with a purpose, and in doing so worship God?
2. What does worshipping God mean to you? Could worship include servicing others?
3. What steps could you take to renew yourself? How would these steps influence your choice of vacation, daily pursuits, and worship patterns?

- **Related Scripture Sources**
    Romans 12:1-2, 21   Philippians 4:8-9
    Philippians 3:20-21   Revelation 21:5

- **New Perspectives**
Consider personal changes you can make and/or new steps you can take to be of service to others.

- **Questions to be Resolved**
(Can be listed on a separate page)

- **A Prayer Thought**

"Glory be to You, Lord God, our Father.

You are the merciful Father, the God from Whom all help comes.

You chose us in Jesus Christ our Lord before the creation of the world.

You rescued us from the power of darkness and brought us safe into the kingdom of Your dear Son.

In our union with Christ You have blessed us with every spiritual blessing in the heavenly world.

You have made us worthy to share in that which You have reserved for Your people in the kingdom of light.

Your love is so great that we may be called the children of God.

Therefore with angels and archangels, and with all the company of heaven, we join in proclaiming the glory of Your name."

Chapter III

God's Love
Transforms

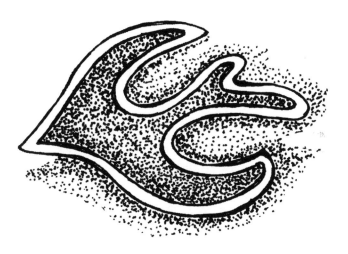

This representation of the dove symbolizes the Holy Spirit and the transformative nature of God's love. God reaches to us, seeking to give us a new life. Recognizing this, St. Paul implored us, "Do not be conformed to this world, but be transformed by the renewing of your minds, so that you may discern what is the will of God – what is good and acceptable and perfect." (Romans 12:2)

In this view of the promise, we see the process of transformation not as an overwhelming assault from the outside. Rather, it is a thrilling – though sometimes painful – unfolding of newness from within. God's promise of transformation is not a demand. It is an invitation from lover to beloved: Come, join yourself to Me; from our togetherness, there will come forth a new creation.

God Calls Us to His Kingdom to Find an Inner Treasure Within Ourselves

The famed Swiss psychologist C.J. Jung had a favorite story he told. The story concerned a monastery in decline after years of unrelenting loss. Inside a handful of aging monks lived lives of dreary routine relieved only by the annual visit of a rabbi to the woods surrounding the monastery.

The abbot of the monastery greeted the rabbi one day. The abbot asked the rabbi why he still came to the woods by the monastery, and he was surprised when the rabbi said he came because the Messiah lived there. The abbot told the others in the monastery what the rabbi had said, and soon everyone was wondering which one in the group was the Messiah.

They began to treat each other with great respect and kindness, thinking any one of them could be Him. As word got around at how the monks treated one another as though each carried divine energy, people came to experience the same thing and the fading monastery became transformed into a thriving, living community once again.

Each of us has at various times in our life been inflicted by low expectations. We become unconscious of our inner world. There is an inner reality within each of us which is like a great treasure lying hidden in the field of our soul waiting to be discovered. When someone finds this inner treasure, and recognizes its value, he/she happily gives up all other goals and ambitions in order to make it real in his/her life. That inner reality within us is referred to by Jesus as the kingdom of Heaven.

A sampling of this truth is referred to in one of Jesus' parables, "Again, the kingdom of Heaven is like a merchant in search of fine pearls; on finding one pearl of great value, he went and sold all that he had and bought it. (Matthew 13:45-46). The importance of the kingdom of Heaven is the central tenet of Jesus' teaching being found frequently in the Gospels. If we know what Jesus meant by the kingdom of God (heaven), we shall be in possession of the keys to His teachings, for everything He said is directly or indirectly related to it.

It is clear that the kingdom is a very personal reality. God has prepared the kingdom for the individual, who may enter it in this lifetime and will discover the kingdom to exist within him/her self. Jesus says, "the kingdom of God is within you." (Luke 17:21)

So the paradox is that the kingdom is both that which we find within ourselves as an inner treasure, and also that which is searching to find us. And when
found, it becomes something of supreme value in the eyes of God. We are the
fine pearls if the kingdom can take root in us, and to such a person God gives a
place of supreme value in His creation. Entrance into and life within the kingdom means the destruction of the old personality with its constricted and un-
creative attitudes. If the kingdom is to come, the old person must die. The new
person is at hand. This is God's call to each person. We come to recognize the
inner world and respond in consciousness to its demands. And we, like the rabbi,
the monks, and the monastery are transformed into a thriving, living, community
once again.

God Calls Us to
His Kingdom to Find
an Inner Treasure Within Ourselves
Reflection/Quest Time

• Exploring Questions for Discussion

1. Were there times in your life when you were inflicted with low expectations, unconscious of your valuable inner world and treasure that lie within? How did you get to this place? How have you gotten out of this place?

2. What attitudes and actions will be evident in a person who believes Jesus' statement that "the kingdom of God is within you"? (Luke 17:21) How might he/she treat others?

• Related Scripture Sources

Matthew 13:45-46	1 Thessalonians 4:7-8
Luke 17:20-24	Isaiah 42:5-9
Acts 2:36-38	Romans 8:28
Matthew 20:16	Romans 14:17-19

• New Perspectives

Consider personal changes you can make and/or new steps you can take to be of service to others.

• Questions to be Resolved

(Can be listed on a separate page)

• A Prayer Thought

"We've a story to tell to the nations, that shall turn their heads to the right,
A story of truth and mercy, a story of peace and light,

We've a Savior to show to the nations, Who the path of sorrow has trod,
That all of the world's great peoples might come to the truth of God.

For the darkness shall turn to dawning, and the dawning to noon-day bright;
And Christ's great kingdom shall come to earth, the kingdom of love and light."

Have You Ever Been Tempted to Just Give Up?

An acquaintance of mine recently flew back east from California. His body was on California time for quite a few days, and he had difficulty catching up on the sleep he had lost. One afternoon, he settled into a comfy chair to rest. Between scenes of an old western movie that he was watching, a 30-second spot appeared on the screen. It caught his attention. In bold letters was the message, "Before you give up, call 555-3242." He dialed the number and found that it was a Christian crisis intervention ministry. The woman's voice on the other end of the line urged him, "Before you give up, try Jesus!" She, then, asked, "Can I be of any help to you?"

My acquaintance thanked her, and indicated that he was a Californian whose only problem was sleeplessness. She laughed, and they had a good conversation about her ministry to people who are about ready to give up.

This experience caused me to reflect on the many people I have met who are hanging on by a thin thread, about to give up. I can see them in my mind's eye: people ready to give up on their marriage after years of trying; others tempted to give up hope for a friend, a child, or loved one; still others who feel that whatever they do to change things, it just doesn't seem to work.

Have you ever felt that way? We all feel it at times. The temptation to give up – on people, relationships, projects, hopes and dreams. Sometimes even on ourselves.

The other day I went into a sporting goods store. It was having a special sale on survival kits for the wilderness camper. While looking through the supplies provided to stay alive when lost or out of touch with civilization, I found a booklet entitled, "Before You Give Up!" It contained 10 things to do to survive. It caused me to ponder what we give people to help them make it when lost or lonely in the wilderness of life today.

The advice to "Try Jesus" may sound too simplistic to many. But, actually, it's quite profound. Faith, as described in the parable of the mustard seed, is God's hope-filled survival kit for each of us. (Matthew 13:31-32) It requires patience, which is in short supply among many of us. When discouraged, we often lament, "if only I had more faith." As if everything depended on the size of our faith, we sometimes spiral into misguided musings about our inadequacy. The bad moods which result drain our energy and spread to people around us like a contagious disease.

Jesus' answer to those who are struggling to keep the faith is piercing and penetrating. He says, before you give-up, consider the parable of the mustard seed. When we are tempted to grow discouraged, we need to remember that it's not the size of our faith but the immensity of God's power that makes all the difference in the world. All we need to do is plant the seed and leave the rest to God.

God is on the move in us. He wants to make us His miracle for the world to see what He can do. And He's certainly not finished with any of us. He's growing a tiny mustard seed of unreserved faith out of you and me. Be sure of that! He has told us He is all-powerful, and that power is available to us. Before you give-up, plant the mustard seed of faith and be ready to be amazed at what God will do.

HAVE YOU EVER BEEN TEMPTED TO JUST GIVE UP?
REFLECTION/QUEST TIME

• **EXPLORING QUESTIONS FOR DISCUSSION**

1. Have you ever felt like giving up? What did you do? How might you have acted differently?

2. When you have felt lost or lonely, what made a difference in helping to overcome it?

3. How could you use your experience to help others?

• **RELATED SCRIPTURE SOURCES**

Matthew 12:31-32   Romans 12:21

John 16:33-17:1-3   John 5:2-5

• **NEW PERSPECTIVES**

Consider personal changes you can make and/or new steps you can take to be of service to others.

• **QUESTIONS TO BE RESOLVED**

(Can be listed on a separate page)

• **A PRAYER THOUGHT**

"Say unto those who are of a fearful heart, be strong and fear not. Behold your God will come and save you. He shall feed His flock like a shepherd. He shall gather the lambs into His arms, and carry them in His bosom."

Called to Service and Love Out of Reverence for God

Each year our nation observes an anniversary of the fateful 9/11 terrorist attacks upon the New York City Twin Towers; Washington, D.C.'s Pentagon; and the doomed plane which brought all of its passengers to their death in western Pennsylvania. A few years ago, our grandson graduated from college in Staten Island, N.Y. We had a family graduation luncheon on the Riverboat Café located in Brooklyn, just across from where the Twin Towers were once located. He recalled, as he looked out the window and as riverboats passed by, the frightful moments when he looked out the window of his freshman dorm four years earlier to see the airplane strike the second tower. The impact of those moments and the tumultuous effects upon his roommate and other new friends in his dorm, whose fathers, uncles and brothers met their fiery fates within the confinement of the Twin Towers, introduced him and all of us to a new reign of a global war of terror. His life, ours, and that of our nation are no longer the same. The costs and consequences are beyond estimation. Clearly, freedom is not free.

Similar generations have experienced different eras of travail and pain. My grandfather served in the Spanish American War. My father was conscripted in World War I. I served overseas in World War II, and my brother was in the Marines during the Korean conflict. Freedom is not free.

When I served a parish in Ohio during the Vietnam conflict, the same kind of notices of wartime fatalities among area youth were appearing in the newspaper, similar to what we have been seeing in our newspapers over the last couple of years. Gold Star mothers, fathers, and spouses are again bearing the pain of these losses.

For two boyhood pals, life was full of promise but everything changed in May 1967 in a place called Vietnam. The fallen were denied promising futures, leaving behind a void which never can be filled in the lives of their grieving families and friends. And not for myself either.

Thomas Alan Johnson and Thomas Alan Ronald had been friends since grade school. Johnson became the seventh person from our country to be killed in Vietnam and Ronald the eighth. They enlisted in the Marine Corps together. They hung out together in town; they played in Little League together. They played football and baseball in high school together, and performed in class plays and chorus together. They went to church camps together, and actively participated in the weekly church youth group. They visited my office and our home regularly for many informal chats, which we commonly called "bull sessions."

I'll never forget the day a military car pulled up to our parsonage one mile outside of a town of 900 people. A Marine colonel came to inform me of Tom Johnson's death in Vietnam, and he requested that I accompany him to Tom's home to inform his parents and family of the death. The grief and the pain were unending. This continued as the family awaited the return of their son's body. I spent lengthy hours and days with the family until the casket arrived from Vietnam. The funeral brought an overwhelming response to the church, as hundreds of sorrowing friends paid their respects. What we did not know that day was that Tom Ronald was already dead too.

The sorrow was compounded 10 days later when the military personnel stopped again at my office to inform me of Tom Ronald's death and again they asked me to accompany them to the home of his parents to deliver the same dreaded message.

During the intervening years, I have gone to the Vietnam War Memorial in Washington, D.C., and I have traced the names of these young men and given the tracings to their families. The local community has also named lanes in their honor: Johnson Lane and Ronald Lane. A baseball park has also been named in Tom Johnson's honor. I have returned to Ohio for the Harvest Home Service of the parish, where I led reunions with families and friends of these fallen heroes. Freedom is not free. In Scripture we are reminded how we should be living in these days of confusion and threatened values. "For it is God's will that by doing right you should silence the ignorance of the foolish. As servants of God, live as free people, yet do not use your freedom as a pretext for evil." (1 Peter 2:15-16). Another translation supplies a freer description by saying, "Exercise your freedom by serving God, not by breaking the rules. Treat everyone you meet with dignity. Love your spiritual family. Revere God. Respect the government." (The Message) God calls us to service and love toward everyone out of our reverence for Him. Let's give it a try. It works.

CALLED TO SERVICE AND LOVE
OUT OF REVERENCE FOR GOD
REFLECTION/QUEST TIME

• EXPLORING QUESTIONS FOR DISCUSSION

1. We are deeply indebted to those who have given their lives so that we can live free. Freedom is truly not free. What does it mean to respond to the admonition in 1 Peter 2:15-18 to "exercise [our] freedom by serving God?" What in specific terms might this service include?

2. How do you interpret the conclusion that God calls us to service and love toward everyone out of our reverence for Him?

3. What are you doing now in your life that identifies you as a servant of God?

• RELATED SCRIPTURE SOURCES

    1 Peter 2:15-16   John 8:33-36

    Galations 5:1

• NEW PERSPECTIVES

Consider personal changes you can make and/or new steps you can take to be of service to others.

• QUESTIONS TO BE RESOLVED

(Can be listed on a separate page)

• A PRAYER THOUGHT

"Deliver us from the sins which lead to war and conflict, and strengthen within us the will to establish righteousness and peace on this earth. Enable us to make use of the world You have entrusted to us."

You Can't Beat the Willing, Welcoming Heart

One of the common greetings we project on one another when we spontaneously meet an acquaintance along the street, at work, in a shopping mall or at church is "Hey, what's new?" Not a bad question when we realize that one of the best ways to get attention or to sell a product is to suggest that what is being offered is new, meaning different or distinct. Another basic curiosity we have is to conjecture about the future. If something involves both, the new and the future, the combination has real impact. Our ears are up.

I am struck by the power of these attractive magnates as I enter a new era in my own vocational life. I am developing an appreciation of what it means to be a pioneer. Beyond regularly teaching college courses in a classroom setting, I have moved into the new frontier of distance learning by offering two credit courses (one regarding ethics and moral problems, and the other regarding death and dying) by means of a tele-web. This means using the combination of television and the internet. Here is a classroom without walls conducted electronically, where teaching, discussions, essays, assignments, tests and grading all take place by way of the technological miracles of the computer and television. Students in this course can literally complete their assignments and participate in the electronic classroom in their pajamas at their convenience. Outstanding luminaries from government, the press, medicine, law, religion, business, and the military join the class by television in grappling with the moral concerns that arise in both personal and professional life. We are dealing in vital ways with the present and the future.

This adventure is new and exciting in being involved with a "journey in" and a "journey out," as we deal with two central questions: "What kind of a person shall I be" and "How shall I live?" Throughout the semester, we focus on the basic issues of what is the right thing to do in life and as we approach death. This leads to intense discussions of human nature and moral decision making. Occasionally, we have some Saturday morning breakfast dialogues with instructor and students to fine tune concepts and issues.

The Bible prominently displays a sense of the new and the future throughout the Old and New Testaments. Transforming ordinary, flawed individuals into new people is the purpose and promise of God's salvation. We catch this theme in spot comments such as, "the Lord creates something new" (Numbers16:30); "He put a new song in my mouth" (Psalms 40:3); and God will "put a new spirit within them" (Ezekiel 11:19). In the New Testament, the development of a new creature involves the power of Christ and what He seeks to do in any one of us. "So if anyone is in Christ, there is a new creation: everything old has passed away." (2 Corinthians 5:17)

If we can be thrilled by new technological advances of communication and the dramatic changes they inspire, why not latch on to the thrill of welcoming and knowing Christ in our hearts? In the new creation foretold by that One who declares that the "first things have passed away" (with this one phrase He sums up all the world's misery of all the ages), because God is "making all things new." In this verse, the Almighty Himself promises that all that now robs life from being fulfilled, joyful, and vibrant will be absent from the transcendent reality to which He is leading history. (Revelation 21:3-5)

Something new! You can't beat God in what He offers to the willing and welcome heart.

You Can't Beat the Willing, Welcoming Heart
Reflection/Quest Time

• **Exploring Questions for Discussion**

1. Transforming ordinary, flawed individuals into new people is the purpose and promise of God's salvation. Can you give witness to a fulfillment of this transformation in your own life and the lives of others? Share this with others.
2. If all things have become new, can you claim a thrill of welcoming and knowing Christ in your heart? When and how do you pass this on to others?
3. Are you aware of what can rob you from being fulfilled, joyful, and vibrant as a faithful disciple? Name some of the forms of evil which block your growth.

• **Related Scripture Sources**

Psalm 40:3   Ezekial 11:19
2 Corinthians 5:17   Revelation 21:5

• **New Perspectives**

Consider personal changes you can make and/or new steps you can take to be of service to others.

• **Questions to be Resolved**

(Can be listed on a separate page)

• **A Prayer Thought**

"With joyfulness and longing we look to You, O Lord;
Receive us in Your mercy, and cheer us with Your Word.
Crown us with love enduring and promises of grace,
And let Your holy blessing remain within this place.

The years have all been crowded with tokens of Your love,
And many who have sought You now worship You above.
But we, O Lord, still need You, our pilgrim feet to stay,
For evil often triumphs, as faith to fear gives way."

STRENGTH MADE PERFECT
IN WEAKNESS

Have you taken a vacation? Time is running out but there is still a basketful of opportunities to enjoy a refreshing change. Enjoy!

Part of August was a vacation time for our extended family set forth in two contrasting models. Model one involved experiencing a week on beautiful Kiawah Island in South Carolina. Kiawah Island is 10 miles of beach and 10,000 acres of semi-tropical beauty complimented by award-winning architecture and landscape planning. Among the delights for a vacationer is championship golf with four resort courses known for their symmetry and design. Tennis courts, paved leisure trails for hiking and bicycling, boating, and swimming are featured activities. Our family of grandparents, parents, and grandchildren enjoyed them all, including also an oyster roast and a side trip to nearby historic Charleston. Most vacationers appeared healthy, energetic, bronzed by the sun, and ready for the next exciting activity.

In coming back home, my wife and I spent a few days in the Poconos at Spruce Lake Retreat Center which sponsored a gathering for families with mentally handicapped members. We were introduced to the theme of the first presentation entitled, Finding Hope in the Midst of Bleak Despair: The audience was made up of loving families, all of whom had at least one mentally handicapped person. Canes and wheelchairs were plentiful. Weakness was a clear presence in the midst of many joys exhibited by those who joined in the programmed activities. Despite handicaps, mini golf, balloon ball volleyball, swimming, paddle boats, parent-child crafts, nature hikes, wall climbing, a concert, and worship were enthusiastically embraced. We became quickly aware that vacations can be enjoyed by the physically and mentally challenged as well as the healthy and the financially or physically fortunate. Exquisite surroundings and circumstances do not automatically assure elegant vacations or whole persons.

Another theme surfaced during our experience at Spruce Lake; it has continued to stimulate deeply rooted discoveries. The words of the Lord revealed by St. Paul ushered forth from one of the testimonials at this conference in the Poconos. "My grace is sufficient for you, for power is made perfect in weakness." The apostle continues, "So, I will boast all the more gladly of my weaknesses, so that the power of Christ may dwell in me." (2 Corinthians 12:9)

This faithful apostle could see how God's grace could transform what was perceived commonly as "bad" into something good in his life. As an early Christian leader, the apostle learned that God could take our weaknesses and use them to demonstrate His power. Paul was affirming that there is nothing that can happen to one of God's children that if we turn to Him with it, He cannot take us from where we are and begin working some good. God doesn't build a wall around us to isolate us from the risk of harm, but He does surround us with a grace that enables us to transform anything that happens to us.

In the midst of those who are experiencing the weaknesses which accompany the mentally handicapped and their caregivers, I witnessed examples of unconditional love both given and received. Simple joys and a relationship of love provided a spectacle of grace. In my moments of doubt and frustration, I envy the security of such simple faith and reliance upon God. It is then that I realize that someone who is considered mentally handicapped is not the one with the handicap. My obligations, my fear, my pride, my circumstances, my privileges all become disabilities, when I do not submit them to Jesus Christ. One day, when the mysteries of heaven are opened, we will all be amazed at how close God really is to our hearts. But the trustful won't be surprised at all.

STRENGTH MADE PERFECT
IN WEAKNESS
REFLECTION/QUEST TIME

• EXPLORING QUESTIONS FOR DISCUSSION
1. The apostle could see how God's grace could transform what was bad into something good in his life. How have you met the challenge?
2. How do you usually react when God seems silent about what you feel is urgent?
3. What do you do to develop or maintain trust in God during times of disillusionment or despair?

• RELATED SCRIPTURE SOURCES

2 Corinthians 12:7-10	Psalm 27:13-14
Philippians 4:13	Hebrews 12:12-14

• NEW PERSPECTIVES
Consider personal changes you can make and/or new steps you can take to be of service to others.

• QUESTIONS TO BE RESOLVED
(Can be listed on a separate page)

• A PRAYER THOUGHT

"Something beautiful, something good;
All my confusion, He understood;
All I had to offer Him was brokenness and strife,
But He made something beautiful of my life."

Is Human Transformation Possible if We Don't Understand Our Actions?

"The devil made me do it." Have you ever muttered this statement? It usually pops out in awkward moments when you suddenly realize that you just did something you didn't want to do. Maybe it involved something such as eating a piece of candy when you knew it was off the diet. Or maybe that simple statement has accompanied some decision-making which is tantalizingly more serious in nature and consequences. Whenever we make this claim, it is an expression of the very essence of the human situation. We know what is right; we want to do what is right, and yet somehow we never do it. We feel ourselves to be a split personality. It is as if two persons are inside one skin. We are pulled in two directions. We know ourselves to be a walking civil war.

St. Paul in his letter to Christians in Rome grappled with the haunting sensation. He wrote, "I do not understand my own actions. For I do not do what I want, but I do the very thing I hate . . . but in fact it is no longer I that do it, but sin that dwells within me . . . Wretched man that I am! Who will rescue me from this body of death?" (Romans 7:15, 17, 24)

We all know this feeling. Seneca talked of "our helplessness in necessary things." He talked about how people hate their sins and love them at the same time. Ovid, the Roman poet, penned his personal experience: "I see the better things, and I approve them but I follow the worse." Jewish understandings refer to men and women as having two natures, two tendencies, two impulses. They call them the Yetser hatab and the Yetser hara. The conviction is that each of us has a good impulse and an evil impulse inside.

Few would doubt that within all of us there is this battle. There are things in man's human nature which answer to the seduction and the temptation of sin. It is part of the human situation that we know the right and do the wrong, that we are never as good as we know we ought to be. It is a part of the human situation that at one and the same time we are haunted by goodness and haunted by sin.

This human condition plays itself out in so many contemporary issues. We see a demonstration of the inadequacy of human knowledge and human resolution. At a time when cigarette smoking is widely known to cause cancer and warnings persist everywhere, teenagers are smoking more. Even though "Just Say No" is a script emphasized at all levels of the school years, the use of addictive drugs continues to rise. Despite our knowledge of the disastrous health consequences from fatty foods, fast food enterprises flourish. Sex education, such as it is, does not seem to make a dent in the skyrocketing teenage pregnancies or the massive presence of venereal diseases. In the presence of the so-called emphasis on wellness programs on college campuses in which alcohol consumption is discouraged (not to mention that laws restrict it), excessive drinking in college settings is significant problem along with attendant date rapes. Knowledge by itself does not make a person a good person. We may know how we ought to act in any given situation, but that is very far from being able to act in such a manner.

Herein is the difference between morality and a living faith. Morality is knowledge of what to do. Living faith is knowledge of Jesus Christ. It is the redeeming knowledge of a person who dwells within, who transforms. When we know Christ, we are able to do what we know we ought to do.

St. Paul had this assurance when he raised the question, "Who will deliver me from this body of death?" Jesus is one who not only knows what is wrong, but who can also put the wrong into right. The human will un-strengthened by Christ is bound to crack. Can we, should we, try to deal with our human condition without God's help? Or would we rather falter as we face the mounting consequences?

Is Human Transformation Possible if We Don't Understand Our Actions?
Reflection/Quest Time

• Exploring Questions for Discussion

1. In what way is your spirit willing and your "flesh weak"? Have you started a spiritual exercise plan?

2. How does knowing Christ make a difference when your sin or the situations that you face are too big for you to handle?

3. How do you feel reading about Paul's conflict in Romans 7:15? Be sure to also read Romans 8:1-17.

• Related Scripture Sources

Romans 7:14-24   Romans 8:1-17

• New Perspectives

Consider personal changes you can make and/or new steps you can take to be of service to others.

• Questions to be Resolved

(Can be listed on a separate page)

• A Prayer Thought

"Glory be to You, Holy Spirit, our Teacher, Guide and Comforter.

We proclaim Your righteousness and praise.

You pour out the love of God into the hearts of all believers, and make their bodies Your holy temples.

By our own reason and strength we cannot believe in Jesus Christ our Lord, or come to Him; but You call us through the Gospel and enlighten us with gifts of grace.

We praise You, together with the Father and the Son, now and forever."

What Wonderful Discovery Has Moved You Toward a Miracle?

Has anything impressed you lately?

Recently I had my imagination stretched to its utmost limits. We are living in a time when wonderful advances in technology and science have reached unexpected heights. I caught a glimpse of this when two representatives of the Good Shepherd Rehabilitation Hospital spoke and put on a demonstration of some of the latest technological developments in the care of the disabled or handicapped. One of the most intriguing features displayed and demonstrated was a two-wheeled vehicle called a Segway.

This two-wheeled miracle contained a motor in each wheel as well as a computer in each. Holding the wheels together was a platform connected to a metal rod with handlebars to give balance. The demonstrator wheeled himself on this agile jitney, in and among tables and chairs occupied by the audience, just by initiating silent mental commands to go forward or backward. I couldn't believe my eyes. No buttons were pushed, no wires connected, no pedals existed. When the presentation concluded, those of us who were interested were invited to go to a wide room to try it out ourselves.

I couldn't resist my awe and curiosity. I headed for the equipment and asked if I could try it. In a moment I was standing on the little mobile platform and asked what I needed to do. The hospital representative said, "Think forward." I did, and off the Segway traveled with me on it. At the other end of the room I thought, "Stop" and this technological wonder stopped and waited for me to think "backward." I did and this responsive technological genius moved in reverse on the basis of my brain waves.

Since then, I saw a guest at the Celtic Fest roam up and down the street on a Segway, watching the opening parade with joy and complete flexibility. What a wonderful step forward in the healthcare of the elderly, the handicapped, or a flamboyant adventurer. We are truly blessed.

As I write, it is "Trick or Treat" night in our town, and I have just finished my joy and duty to hand out to our house visitors our treat of caramel apples sprinkled with peanuts. On this night, I couldn't figure out why we had such an influx of children visiting our home. We ran out of caramel apples early, after distributing dozens and dozens of these seasonal treats. Upon investigation, I discovered a man out in front of our house using a cell phone giving instructions to drivers of cars on how to get to our house. He also had a commercial flashlight guiding cars filled with children to our home, much like airport technicians guide airplanes into their berths at the end of the runway. So much for the benefits of communication technology such as cell phones that seemed to have invaded our universe!

What wonderful discovery has moved you lately into a technological wonderland? Even more to the point, have you stopped long enough to be fascinated or in awe of any dramatic spiritual transformation in someone's life, perhaps your own? God is in the technology of transforming broken lives. As a matter of fact, wonderful personal transformations are the most significant phenomena of all. It takes a miracle to turn some of us around, in order to find a fulfilling direction in our lives. God-induced changes of attitudes, lifestyles, behavior, addictions, relationships, habits, hatreds, anger, abuse, dishonesty, falsehoods, promiscuity, or racial prejudice are gifts of grace. As the songwriter states, "When He saved my soul, cleansed and made me whole, it took a miracle of love and grace."

The psalmist suggests in Psalm 145:4-5, "One generation shall laud Your works to another, and shall declare Your mighty acts. On the glorious splendor of Your majesty, and on Your wondrous works, I will meditate." This is an opportunity to call "time out" and consider God's unfolding purpose for your life. When God gets a chance, a touch of eternity can become a reality.

WHAT WONDERFUL DISCOVERY
HAS MOVED YOU TOWARD A MIRACLE?
REFLECTION/QUEST TIME

• EXPLORING QUESTIONS FOR DISCUSSION

1. Have you stopped long enough to be fascinated or in awe of any dramatic spiritual transformation in someone's life, perhaps your own?

2. If it takes a miracle to turn some of us around to find a new direction in our lives, are you willing to give God a chance?

3. Is this an opportunity to call "time out" and consider God's unfolding purpose for your life?

• RELATED SCRIPTURE SOURCES

Psalm 145:4-5   2 Corinthians 3:17-18
Romans 12:2

• NEW PERSPECTIVES

Consider personal changes you can make and/or new steps you can take to be of service to others.

• QUESTIONS TO BE RESOLVED

(Can be listed on a separate page)

• A PRAYER THOUGHT

"God of creation, whose love invites all people to receive the blessing reserved for us since before time began,

Grant ears of faith, that each one may clearly hear Your gracious call.

God of salvation, whose love encompasses all humanity, who assumed flesh and blood and died that all might live,

Give eyes of faith, Lord Jesus, that everyone may plainly see You among us.

God of inspiration, whose love initiates new ways of reaching out to all who risk believing.

Guide our lives in faith, that we may willingly become Your instruments of love and truth."

GIVE YOUR PERSONALITY
A SPIRIT LIFT

"It's changed my personality!" That was the confident claim of an middle-aged entertainer who had just had a facelift. She had gone to a world-renowned cosmetic surgeon. His artistry had removed the lines that plowed deeply into her cheeks, suggesting advanced age and years of difficulties. The bags under her eyes also had been removed, and with a careful incision along the hairline, the surgeon was able to stretch out the furrows in her brow.

The woman looked 15 years younger. The harried, pressured look her face had developed was gone. "You look like a new woman," the TV interviewer said, in affirmation of the pain and expense she had endured.

"I only hope I can stay this way!" she responded in a concerned voice which contracted her smooth, China-doll face.

"What do you mean?" the TV host asked, immediately sensing her anxiety about the possible impermanence of her mask-like cosmetic transformation.

"Well, the surgeon tells me that plastic surgery and face lifts last only if there is a change in my inner patterns of thought and feelings. He says that my face is an expression of my psyche, and that I'll look the way I did again in three years unless I learn how to live. He recommended that I see a psychologist or a spiritual adviser to get a soul-lift that will help me keep my facelift."

Amazing! The surgery had altered the woman's appearance enough to give her a temporary positive self-image, but it had not really changed her personality. It would take more than a facelift to make her a new person. A change in her personality would be necessary to do that.

Personality change is not easy. Most of us are what the patterns of learning and experience have made us. We are conditioned creatures. Personality is the sum total of our individuality. It is the outward expression of the person within each of us – that which characterizes and distinguishes us.

The people around us know who we are through our personalities. Personality is the observable "I." Environment, education, culture, significant people and experience have all had a sculpting hand in shaping the clay of our personality. We are all in the process of developing our personalities around the picture of the person we envision ourselves to be.

The person we are inside will irrevocably control the personality we express outwardly to others. Any change in our personality must be the result of a transformation of the values, goals, feelings, attitudes, and self-esteem of the person who lives inside our skins.

That is where Jesus begins. He can transform our personalities. He never used the word. It cannot be found in the Scriptures. Yet everything Jesus said, did, and can do in our individual lives alters the character and shapes the personality. He has called us to be His people in order to remold us in His own image and then send us into life as liberated personalities. What He does for us is in preparation for what He waits to do through us in the world.

The parable of the leaven (yeast) is the parable of the transformation of personality. Jesus tells us how the Gospel can get into us, and then how we are to get the Gospel into the world. "The kingdom of Heaven is like yeast that a woman took and mixed in with three measures of flour until all of it was leavened." (Matthew 13:33)

I'm not a baker, but I have occasionally made a loaf of fresh bread using a bread-maker. Every loaf, every slice, smells and tastes so good, and it seems to be a miracle. During Biblical times, leaven was a little piece of dough which had been saved from a previous baking. Today we call it "starter," and we just open a little package and pour it into our bread-making machine along with a packaged mix. During the night, it does its thing and in the early morning the house is filled with a beautiful aroma. From inside the machine emerges a magnificent loaf of bread. The leaven does a miraculous job of creation. It works inadvertently.

The more we focus our total attention on the leavening Lord, the more we become like the Lord. Our task is not to try to develop special virtue, but to yield ourselves to Christ. Christ-likeness grows naturally.

The leaven of God took charge of the disciples and made them apostles. The Lord became a transforming energy within. Christ's power to change personality was especially evident in Saul, the executioner, as he became Paul, the transformed, with a compelling message.

The parable of the leaven is both confrontation and cheer. It confronts us with what Christ wants to do in our lives, and cheers us with the good news that no one needs to remain as he or she is.

Where is the leaven at work in you right now? For whom have you been called to be an agent of leavening? Christ has transformed every part of us, every person around us and all of society.

GIVE YOUR PERSONALITY A SPIRIT LIFT
REFLECTION/QUEST TIME

• **EXPLORING QUESTIONS FOR DISCUSSION**

1. Is the person you are inside controlling the personality you express outwardly to others? Are the results positive or negative? Why? Do you seek a change?

2. Any changes in our personality must be the result of a transformation of the values, goals, feelings, attitudes, and self esteem of the person who lives inside our skins. Is Christ-likeness growing naturally in you?

3. For whom have you been called to be an agent of leavening?

• **RELATED SCRIPTURE SOURCES**

    Matthew 13:33   Acts 9:10-22
    1 Corinthians 5:6-8

• **NEW PERSPECTIVES**

Consider personal changes you can make and/or new steps you can take to be of service to others.

• **QUESTIONS TO BE RESOLVED**

(Can be listed on a separate page)

• **A PRAYER THOUGHT**

"God of creation, whose love invites all people to receive the blessing reserved for us since before time began.

Grant ears of faith, that each one may clearly hear Your gracious call.

God of salvation, whose love encompasses all humanity, who assumed flesh and blood and died that all might live.

Give eyes of faith, Lord Jesus, that everyone may plainly see You among us.

God of inspiration, whose love initiates new ways of reaching out to all who risk believing.

Guide our lives in faith, that we may willingly become Your instruments of love and truth."

BELIEVING TRULY MEANS
DYING TO THINGS WE LOVE MOST

My wife and I have experienced the process of moving periodically. This is not new to us. In serving parishes in four different states, moving is part of the pastoral experience. But this time it is different. The move involves a great reduction of our possessions. This change means giving up favorite things that we have accumulated over a lifetime, in order to take up residence in much smaller apartment space. Our personal library, which fills many bookshelves, is gradually being distributed to interested recipients. We have discovered that the reduction and the elimination of previous treasures has become for us like the process of death. Decision by decision, we come face to face with the issues of "What do we really love?" and "What do we really need?" It suggests one of the basic questions of life, "What is Real?"

Margery Williams in her book, *The Velveteen Rabbit* designed for children but also very alive for adults leads us to a touching and penetrating discussion of what it means to be real: "The Skin Horse had lived longer in the nursery than any of the others. He was so old that his brown coat was bald in patches and showed the seams underneath, and most of the hairs in his tail had been pulled out to string bead necklaces. He was wise, for he had seen a long succession of mechanical toys arrive to boast and swagger, and by-and-by break their mainsprings and pass away, and he knew that they were only toys, and would never turn into anything else. For nursery magic is very strange and wonderful, and only those playthings that are old and wise and experienced like the Skin Horse understand all about it."

"What is REAL?" asked the [Velveteen] Rabbit one day, when they were lying side by side near the nursery fender, before Nana came to tidy the room. "Does it mean having things that buzz inside you and a stick-out handle?"

"Real isn't how you are made," said the Skin Horse. "It's a thing that happens to you. When a child loves you for a long, long time, not just to play with, but REALLY loves you, then you become Real."

"Does it hurt?" asked the Rabbit.

"Sometimes," said the Skin Horse, for he was always truthful. "When you are Real you don't mind being hurt."

"Does it happen all at once, like being wound up," he asked, "or bit by bit?"

"It doesn't happen all at once," said the Skin Horse. "You become. It takes a long time. That's why it doesn't often happen to people who break easily, or have sharp edges, or who have to be carefully kept. Generally, by the time you are

Real, most of your hair has been loved off, and your eyes drop out and you get loose in the joints and very shabby. But these things don't matter at all, because once you are Real you can't be ugly, except to people who don't understand."

It takes time and love and faith to become real. Only very late do we learn the price of the risk of believing, because only very late do we face up to the idea of death. This is what is difficult: believing truly means dying. Dying to everything: to our reasoning, to our childhood dreams, to our attachment to earthly things. This is why faith is so difficult. It is so difficult to hear from Jesus a cry of anguish for us and our difficulties in believing, "Oh, if only you could believe!" (John 3:12)

Because not even He can take our place in the leap of faith; it is up to us. It is like dying! It is up to us, and no one else is able to take our place.

The truest and greatest prototype of this act of faith that we, as the People of God, possess is the Biblical account of the trial of Abraham. God said, "Take your son, your only son Isaac, whom you love, and go to the land of Moriah, and offer him there as a burnt offering on one of the mountains that I shall show you. So Abraham rose early in the morning, saddled his donkey, and took two of his young men with him, and his son Isaac." (Genesis 22:2-3) That act required a leap of faith on Abraham's part! It was a very personal act, and it was an act of death.

Without love, it is impossible to understand God's command to Abraham. God wants to communicate with the depths of Abraham's being and to tear him from himself and his involvement with his own problems, which are like self-centered possessions; God wants to make this creature of His "more His", this man who is destined not for the tents of earth but for those of Heaven.

An act of pure faith is the death of what we love most. And God has set the example. "For God so loved the world that He gave His only Son, so that everyone who believes in Him may not perish but may have eternal life." (John 3:16). If you are ready to become real, let God's love settle in. God loves you and will make you "Real."

BELIEVING TRULY MEANS
DYING TO THINGS WE LOVE MOST
REFLECTION/QUEST TIME

• **EXPLORING QUESTIONS FOR DISCUSSION**
1. Has there been a time in your life when you had to give up some favorite things that you have accumulated over a lifetime? How did you resolve the following questions: "What do I really love?" "What do I really need?" "What really matters?" "What is real?"
2. Do you think living a "real" life involves a degree of dying to everything of earthly value?
3. Are you ready to become "real?"

• **RELATED SCRIPTURE SOURCES**

John 3:12   Proverbs 11:3-6
Genesis 2:2   Genesis 20:5-7

• **NEW PERSPECTIVES**
Consider personal changes you can make and/or new steps you can take to be of service to others.

• **QUESTIONS TO BE RESOLVED**
(Can be listed on a separate page)

• **A PRAYER THOUGHT**

"Have Thine own way, Lord! Have Thine own way!
Thou art the potter, I am the clay!
Mold me and make me, After Thy will,
While I am waiting, Yielded and still.

Have Thine own way, Lord! Have Thine own way!
Wounded and weary, Help me, I pray!
Power, all power, Surely is Thine!
Touch me and heal me, Savior divine!

Have Thine own way, Lord! Have Thine own way!
Hold o'er my being, Absolute sway!
Fill with Thy Spirit, Til all shall see,
Christ only, always, Living in me!"

(HYMN 400, VERSES 1, 3, 4, HYMNS FOR THE FAMILY OF GOD)

Chapter IV
God's Love
Endures

God's love for His creation never wanes. Our faith ought to be anchored in the confidence of these assurances: "We have this hope, a sure and steadfast anchor of the soul, a hope that enters the inner shrine behind the curtain." (Hebrews 6:19) "For the Lord is good; His steadfast love endures forever; and His faithfulness to all generations." (Psalm 100:5) "The word of the Lord endures forever." (1 Peter 1:25). Love "endures all things." (1 Corinthians 13:7)

God's Love Found in the Gift of a Childhood Train

Our family recently moved into a new apartment which is greatly downsized from our previous residences. Through the years as a hobby, I have collected and erected various model railroad setups which have been prominent living room attractions in our home over the Christmas holidays. House guests and visitors got a chance to put on an engineer's hat and run the railroad. This year, however, space limitations have made it necessary for me to pick just one of my trains to display and to place it in some inconspicuous place.

The track oval now weaves its way under and through the legs of my desk. My train of choice is my childhood Lionel O-Gauge unit which includes an engine, a few coal cars, and a caboose that I received at Christmas about 60 years ago during the heart of the financial depression. For me this little electric train captures a host of memories and a tremendous message of love.

My father was a carpenter and times were tough when I was growing-up. Work opportunities were scarce and income was sporadic and unpredictable. Frequently my dad was paid for his skills and services by those who had little money with baskets of potatoes, large metal containers of milk, baskets of apples, or a few chickens. This meant that Christmas gifts were few, inexpensive, and usually items of clothing which were needed.

To expect an electric train for Christmas was relegated to the level of fantasy experienced in paging through the Sears Roebuck catalog. However, one Christmas, a Lionel train set appeared beyond all belief. It didn't take my mother long before she explained that my father put this train on layaway at a local store and paid $1.00 over a couple of months in order to have it paid for by Christmas time. I was and still am ecstatic over the train and very proud of my father.

At the moment, two bulbs on the front and back end of the engine are missing and I have been in search at stores for replacements. In order to get the right size, I have carried the engine in my hands from store to store in hopes of making my train set complete. Carrying the engine has inspired all kinds of attention and loads of comments. One teenager at the checkout counter called my little engine "awesome." A man stopped in an aisle and offered to buy it for "big bucks." Another observer told me, "You have something special there." I wish that my father was still living and that he could have walked with me through the stores to see the glances and hear the comments.

For me, in a sense, my little childhood train is bigger than life. It models a lifelong understanding of what love and sacrifice look like. It typifies my father, who modeled over and over again what a dad can mean in giving and providing a guiding light. In truth my train embodies my father's nurture and love.

In reality, this is the message of Christmas. We call it the Incarnation, when God enters our world. Christ is the incarnation of God. In Him, we are encountered by a God who loves us so much that He took upon Himself our flesh, our humanity, our world, our troubles, in order to bring us to Himself. In assuming our flesh, God ennobles and lifts up our lives, and He shows us humanity at its finest.

The Scriptures describe this in several ways. In the Gospel of John (1:14) we read "And the Word became flesh and lived among us, and we have seen His glory, the glory of a father's only son, full of grace and truth." St. Paul suggests, "For in Him all the fullness of God pleased to dwell, and through Him God was pleased to reconcile to Himself all things." (Colossians 1:19-20)

In this baby, born to Mary and Joseph, we have seen as much of God as we ever hope to see. When one thinks about it, this is wondrous good news. We can cast out our sin, let the Savior in, and the world is set right side up.

God's Love Found in the
Gift of a Childhood Train
Reflection/Quest Time

• **Exploring Questions for Discussion**
1. What gifts that you have received have been especially meaningful?
2, Have you ever found God's presence outside of worship?
3. The Gospel of John underscores Jesus' true identity through the titles He is given – the Word; the Only Begotten Son; the Lamb of God; the Son of God; the True Bread of Life; the Resurrection; the Vine; the Bread of Life; the Light of the World; the Good Shepherd; the Way, the Truth, and the Life. What do these titles for Jesus tell us about the Word becoming flesh?

• **Related Scripture Sources**

John 1:1-14   Colossians 1:15-19

John 20:30-31   John 1-2

• **New Perspectives**
Consider personal changes you can make and/or new steps you can take to be of service to others.

• **Questions to be Resolved**
(Can be listed on a separate page)

• **A Prayer Thought**

"Jesus Christ is the eternal Word, Who was made flesh and dwelt among us.

Those who are His beheld His glory, the glory of the Only Begotten of the Father, full of grace and truth.

In Him, dwells all the fullness of the Godhead bodily. He is the true God and eternal life."

GIVE ME A SURPRISE OF LIFE BUT HOLD THE PROBLEMS PLEASE

Our family, including grandparents, parents, and grandchildren, is still experiencing after-glow following our recent summer vacation together in the state of Maine and Acadia National Park. There we found soaring granite cliffs side by side with sand and cobblestone beaches. Glacier-carved mountains reared up from the sea, cupping deep lakes in the valleys. We also discovered meadowlands, marshes, and dense evergreen forests. Everywhere the ocean made its presence felt, whether by sight, sound, or smell. Acadia encompasses more than 40,000 acres providing hiking, biking, fishing, carriage rides, boat cruises, kayaking, and rock-bound enclosures, cozy for reflection or scenic photographs. Our family adventure included them all, beginning with a boat cruise which guaranteed seeing puffins and whales.

Unfortunately, the day we chose to cruise and see what we had never seen before was rainy, foggy and cold. The sea was rough. Puffins are the cutest member of the family of arctic sea birds named out of the silly way they puff out their chests when they walk. They achieve the amazing speed of 48 to 55 MPH, when they fly and flap their wings up to 400 beats a minute. Regrettably, we never got to see them in their habitat at the rock-bound base of a well-known lighthouse because of a dense fog. In fact, we couldn't see the lighthouse. It was desolate with high winds, fog and powerful waves. By the time we arrived at this location about forty percent of the passengers were seasick, including most of our family. The cruise went on in search of whales with the same results. Everyone aboard was wishing for the nightmare to end. Upon return to shore, the cruise staff refunded fifty percent of the ticket fare because of the futile results. For our family, it was a challenge to go on to experience a delightful vacation, despite the troublesome beginnings. Later that week, others enjoyed an identical ocean cruise where they saw the beautiful, enduring puffins, and the spectacular whales.

Life has disappointing moments for all of us, when satisfaction, success, dreams, and health elude us and even God seems distant. Jesus warned us that we would have problems in the world. (John 16:33) No one is immune to pain or insulated from suffering, and no one gets to skate through life problem free. Life is a series of problems. Not all of them are big, but all are significant in God's growth process for you and me.

In the Bible, we discover Peter, who assures us that problems are normal. He states: "Beloved, do not be surprised at the fiery ordeal that is taking place among you to test you, as though something strange were happening to you." (1 Peter 4:12) God can use problems to draw us closer to Him. The Bible reminds us that "Truly the eye of the Lord is on those who fear Him, on those who hope in His steadfast love, to deliver their soul from death, and to keep them alive in famine." (Psalm 34: 18-19) We learn things about God in suffering that we can't learn any other way. God could have kept Joseph out of jail (Romans 12:21), kept Daniel out of the lion's den (Daniel 6:16-23), kept Jeremiah from being tossed into a slimy pit (Jeremiah 36:6), kept Paul from being shipwrecked three times (2 Corinthians 11:25), and kept the three young Hebrew men from being thrown into the blazing furnace (Daniel 3:1-26). But He didn't! He let those problems happen, and every one of those persons was drawn close to Him as a result.

Problems force us to look past ourselves and depend upon God. The Apostle Paul testified to this benefit. "Indeed, we felt that we had received the sentence of death so that we would rely not on ourselves but on God who raises the dead. He who rescued us from deadly peril will continue to rescue us." (2 Corinthians 1:9-10) You and I will never know that God is all we need until God is all we got. Everything that happens to us has spiritual significance. Our family learned quickly that there was something more than puffins and whales which can put together a significant vacation. What will it take for each of us to be focused on God's presence and His unfolding purpose, especially when He feels distant?

Give Me a Surprise of Life
but Hold the Problems Please
Reflection/Quest Time

• Exploring Questions for Discussion
1. Consider a few of the problems you are facing in your life now. Does God seem distant or near?
2. What steps can you take to bring God closer?
3. What might be the purpose of personal problems in God's unfolding purpose for your life?

• Related Scripture Sources

1 Peter 4:12	2 Corinthians 1:9
Jeremiah 38:6	Romans 12:21
Psalm 34:18	David 3:1-26
2 Corinthians 11:25	Daniel 6:16-23

• New Perspectives
Consider personal changes you can make and/or new steps you can take to be of service to others.

• Questions to be Resolved
(Can be listed on a separate page)

• A Prayer Thought

"Lord, You have kept the promise You made to our ancestors, and have come to the help of Your servant people.

You remembered to show mercy to Abraham and Sarah and to all their descendants forever!

We praise You, Lord. You are enthroned in glory, yet You came and continue to come for all who will receive You. We praise You, for You are good, and Your mercy endures forever."

A MOTHER'S WORDS
TO LIVE BY

We come annually to Mother's Day, originally established by President Woodrow Wilson as a day to recognize the role of mothers in our lives. The day is acknowledged in countless ways, but it is customarily celebrated with accolades of flowers, choice chocolates, meal settings among the generations, and recognitions of families within the worship centers of the nation. For many of us, memories loom large, sparked with favorite and decisive experiences cultivated by loving mothers who were more than the biological source of our life. They rocked our cradles. More importantly they cuddled our dreams and inspired our aspirations. Mothers of the world are known for giving and giving again to the futures of their offspring in sacrifices that mold character and assist in success.

For me, my mother was one of these special people. One of my earliest recollections was the time when I came home from visiting a neighborhood playmate during the Depression years. I was wearing a wristwatch. My mother noticed it immediately and asked where I got it. I told her, "George gave it to me. It was one of three he had and he didn't need it." Her response was clear and deliberate. "Take that watch back to George. We can't afford to buy you one but it doesn't belong to you." It was a slow depressing walk back to George's home but it was a lesson for a lifetime.

I also remember the small sitting stool in our family kitchen not far from the cookie jar, where I frequently sat after school enjoying a snack and glass of milk, while my mother prepared the evening meal. I recognize it now as a seat of learning, a place from which I recalled the joys and/or disappointments of the day at school, in sports, or at social events while my mother listened intently. She knew how to be hot or cold in her responses, depending on whether I needed comfort or caution, commendation or reproof.

In the midst of motherly advice and understanding would come some recurring themes, depending on what was I needed. Among the family proverbs were:

"A good name is to be chosen rather than great riches." (Proverbs 22:1)
"A soft answer turns away wrath." (Proverbs 15:1)
"Wine is a mocker, strong drink a brawler." (Proverbs 20:1)

During our teenage years when we were so busy in youthful activities, my mother placed a plaque on the wall next to the front door reminding us of the Biblical exhortation, "Those who wait for the Lord shall renew their strength, they shall mount up with wings like eagles, they shall run and not be weary, they shall walk and not faint." (Isaiah 40:31)

What my mother taught was exemplified even more by what was caught from her example. Despite her limited eighth grade education, she partnered with my father in managing the office of his contracting business, took in boarders to augment our family income, sponsored music lessons for her three children, and took us camping on summer vacations. She and my father somehow managed to be beside the gangplank of the ships in the New York harbor in order to greet me when I returned home from military service in Africa and Europe. She arranged for me to start college just two days later. In ensuing years, she followed her grandchildren in their athletics and school events.

Through it all, God and faith commitment were much more than an accessory to her. Regular worship with our entire family was central and paramount as she practiced what she represented in her 91 years of life.

Peter Marshall in his prayer as chaplain of the U.S. Senate offered this appropriate sentiment: "On this day of sacred memories, our Father, we would thank Thee for our mothers who gave us life, who surrounded us early and late with love and care, whose prayers on our behalf still cling around the Throne of Grace, a haunting perfume of love's petitions."

Happy Mother's Day!

A Mother's Words to Live By
Reflection/Quest Time

• **Exploring Questions for Discussion**

1. Can you recall some specific sayings or cautions which your mother emphasized as you grew up? Write them down. How did you feel about them then? And now?

2. How have these teachings affected your life course?

3. How was God present in your family when you were growing up? Was He present in the expression of your mother's love or someone else's example?

• **Related Scripture Sources**

Proverbs 22:1	Proverbs 15:1
John 19:27	Proverbs 20:1
Isaiah 40:31	

• **New Perspectives**

Consider personal changes you can make and/or new steps you can take to be of service to others.

• **Questions to be Resolved**

(Can be listed on a separate page)

• **A Prayer Thought**

"Comfort us in our brokenness and give us grace to claim our relationship as Your children.

Life-giving Spirit, You came in power to form and guide the church, a family with varied gifts and graces. Grant that church and home may model for each other the nurturing of individuals and the growth of community. We recognize the difficulty of forming family with those who are different from ourselves, and with those who are like ourselves. We confess our failure to love and grow, our impatience for others to change, our blindness to one another's needs. Yet we rejoice that You have given us each other, and we dedicate ourselves to mutual support and love, trusting not in our own strength, but in Your strong compassion.

Bless and guide us, Triune God, and enable us to support and love each other."

War Memorials Can Motivate Us to be "Instruments of Peace"

Recently I visited the nation's capital, and I had an opportunity to see the cherry blossoms in their full beauty. What a beautiful spectacle! Our delegation of four also visited the United States Holocaust Memorial Museum as well as the Vietnam War Memorial Wall. What a contrast. The blossoms spoke eloquently of beauty and life. The memorial sites amplified ugliness and death.

All of us experience defining moments in our lives. Many times these moments come as surprises. While our trip to Washington D.C. was planned specifically to coincide with cherry blossom time and to include visits to the war memorials of two separate generations, the impact was not what we had expected. Our visit reminded us of experiences that profoundly affected us.

The Holocaust Museum gave mute evidence to the sacrifice and destruction of Hitler's Nazi regime in the slaughter of six million European Jews. These atrocities were taking place while I was in my teens and most of the world was unaware of the demonic dimensions of Hitler's conquests among his various human targets – the ill, the intellectuals, the disabled, the Slavs and the Jews. He strove toward the ultimate rule of the German master race over what he perceived to be subordinate people. My trip to the Holocaust Museum painfully reminded me again of these inhumanities which were being fully disclosed when I was a G.I. in Europe.

The Vietnam War Memorial portrayed the thousands of youth whose lives were snuffed out on remote battlefields. My personal interest during my visit to the Memorial was to pay my respects to two 18-year-old sons of our church and community whose funerals I conducted while a pastor in Ohio. They both were killed by hostile enemy fire within two weeks of each other. I shall never forget the deep emotions I experienced in joining the army major who asked me to accompany him to bear the dreaded news to their families. Powerful emotions revisited me as I located the names of each of these young men on the surface of the Memorial wall. All along the wall were others who were also expressing their kinship and remembrance of loved ones lost in battle.

Internal review in the presence of senseless suffering can incubate a new sense of intimate identification with those who suffer. We can draw near to their suffering with an awareness that paves the way to a new purpose for our lives. Saint Paul expresses something of his personal quest to make sense of the complexities of life by declaring his hope: "I want to know Christ and the power of His resurrection and the sharing of His sufferings by becoming like Him in death, if somehow I may attain the resurrection from the dead." (Philippians 3:10-11)

At a time when disturbing overtures of group hatred, and racial and ethnic hostilities show their ugly faces here in our country and around the world, we need to respond with new personal diligence and devotion. We are never that far away from atrocities and death. We need to nourish anew our spiritual resources. God's word to love is never out of date. Our resolve can be like the Psalmist who said, "I treasure Your word in my heart, so that I may not sin against You . . . I will meditate on Your precepts, and fix my eyes on Your ways. I will delight in Your statutes; I will not forget Your word." (Psalm 119:11, 15-16)

May the power of Christ's resurrection stimulate us to explore God's transforming power in being a new creature with a new witness. So much of our common life is in need of a new birth. Our neighbors, our colleagues at work, our schools, our nation, and our world await the blessings which come in a fellowship of suffering. How can we find the peace which only Christ can give, and in turn become "instruments of peace?"

War Memorials Can Motivate Us to be "Instruments of Peace"
Reflection/Quest Time

• **Exploring Questions for Discussion**

1. The presence of evil and good is ever with us. What are the causes of conflict which have led us in every generation into bloodshed and human brokenness?

2. Can we define peace which passes all understanding in Christ Jesus?

3. How might we act as "instruments of peace" in our homes, churches, and communities?

• **Related Scripture Sources**

Philippians 3:10   Luke 2:14
Psalm 122:7   Luke 19:41-42
Isaiah 26:3   2 Corinthians 13:11-14

• **New Perspectives**

Consider personal changes you can make and/or new steps you can take to be of service to others.

• **Questions to be Resolved**

(Can be listed on a separate page)

• **A Prayer Thought**

"Peace, perfect peace, by thronging do these pressed?
To do the will of Jesus, this is rest."

Becoming an Instrument
of Peace in a
Violent Generation

We have a new guest at our house. Over the past 20 years, there has been a steady flow of international visitors with whom we have had the privilege of sharing homegrown hospitality. But this new arrival, now much at home in our backyard, is different. He feels very comfortable in our backyard, serving as a bird bath and breakfast statuary, almost a shrine to our neighborhood variety of birds.

Our guest is a woodcarving of St. Francis of Assisi bearing a flowing monk's garb adorned by a few wood-carved birds on his shoulder and arms. He holds a tray occupied with two clay bowls, one for bird seed and the other for water. Francis, our life-size carving, is a daily reminder to us of one of our favorite persons of history who sought to imitate the life of Christ and to carry out so totally Christ's work in Christ's way. As part of this commitment he became known as a lover of nature, a social worker, an itinerant preacher, and a lover of poverty.

We became acquainted with Francis, our backyard guest, when my wife and I visited our favorite birdseed store. He stood outside the front of the store as if to greet the customers as they approached the entrance. My wife thought he would make a perfect Mother's Day gift, and so St. Francis came home with us. In the meantime he made a rather circuitous route on his way to New Jersey before being placed in our backyard. Realizing that the portable statuary of St. Francis would make a good focus of attention for a Junior Sermon, I took him to a morning church service where he was used as a prop for the "Children's Chat" portion of the service. To get to this church in Palmyra, New Jersey, one travels on the turnpike and also crosses a toll bridge. It was at the toll booth of each of these travel points that curiosity ran high. St. Francis was placed across the back of our van elevated over a folded rear seat. When I turned on the interior light as I reached for my toll money and tickets, the toll keeper became distracted as his eyes fastened on my reclining guest. Immediately he lost count of his change as he inquired, "Is he all right?" and I replied facetiously, "O yes, I had him embalmed." He continued his inquiry, "Where are you going?" and "Who is he?" I assured the toll taker that he was St. Francis. Our van moved on to our destination, each time with the expectation that some state trooper would be stopping us for further investigation. Fortunately, this did not happen.

How appropriate that our backyard carving of St. Francis traveled like an itinerant before setting on our lawn. In real life, St. Francis of Assisi wandered for years through towns and villages living in absolute poverty preaching the Gospel. In rags, he mingled with beggars and with a kiss he related to lepers. His aim in his new life driven by a vision of Christ was to walk in the Savior's footsteps and be obedient to the charge given in Matthew 10:9-10, "Take no gold, or silver, or copper in your belts, no bag for your journey, or two tunics, or sandals, or a staff."

This humble servant was a constant instrument of peace amid the rampant violence and carnage of his age, in the early 1200's, throughout a good part of Europe as well as Morocco and Tunisia in Africa. Blood vendettas, legal mutilations, city strife, incessant war, murder, and troubling moral conditions in the Church were a part of everyday life. Medieval towns had thick walls and fortifications which offered protection from roving bands of mercenaries. St. Francis applied his life of contemplation and prayer to the practical urgencies of his violent time in history.

This close imitation of Christ, still eight centuries after his passing, continues to intrigue and sometimes discomfort. The thousands who have followed the model of St. Francis have made a forceful impact then and now. Much of what he faced then we are facing now. Ours is a violent generation. We ought to be inspired by his example.

BECOMING AN INSTRUMENT OF PEACE IN A VIOLENT GENERATION
REFLECTION/QUEST TIME

• EXPLORING QUESTIONS FOR DISCUSSION
1. Have there been figures in your life that have shaped its course? Who? Why?
2. How might the model set forth by St. Francis inspire your walk with Christ?

• RELATED SCRIPTURE SOURCES

Matthew 10:9-11   Isaiah 61:3
Philippians 2:1-4   Hebrews 6:13-20

• NEW PERSPECTIVES
Consider personal changes you can make and/or new steps you can take to be of service to others.

• QUESTIONS TO BE RESOLVED
(Can be listed on a separate page)

• A PRAYER THOUGHT

"Is not this the kind of worship that pleases Me, says our God: to undo the bonds of injustice, to let the oppressed go free and break every yoke, to share bread with the hungry and shelter the homeless poor, to clothe the naked and not turn from your own people? I was hungry and You fed me, thirsty and You gave me drink, a stranger and You welcomed me, naked and You clothed me, sick or in prison and You visited me.

When did we see You hungry and feed You, thirsty and give You drink? When did we see You a stranger and welcome You, naked and clothe You, sick or in prison and visit You?

Truly, I say to You, when You did it to one of the least of these, You did it to Me."

Let The Church Go To Hell

"Let the Church go to Hell." I recently saw this catchy statement on a church signboard in Columbus, Ohio. It stopped me in my tracks. I wondered what exactly was meant by it. The most obvious meaning is clear, especially considering the way the church is often ignored or neglected at times. Some people would prefer if the church literally went to Hell.

However, the pastor who put this statement in front of his church explained that it meant that wherever wrongness or sin exists, Christ's church ought to be present, working to provide comfort and to heal brokenness.

Is this actually happening in your church and in the living-out of your faith?

I have been struck by the continual collision between Christ and our culture, between the church and our world. In fact, for anyone standing with one foot in the world and one foot in the church, it becomes a difficult problem to keep one's footing.

The more honestly we look at ourselves, the more we realize that we are often guilty of giving our warm endorsement to such teachings as the Ten Commandments or the Sermon on the Mount while not making great strides to abide by them. What might an examination of our faith reveal? Can a faith unapplied actually survive?

Sadly, a gap often exists between our public creed and our personal creed. The Apostles' Creed, pronounced during each worship service, is the Christian church's official statement of faith. But, I have become convinced that many of us have privately dedicated ourselves to another creed. And it might be stated thus:

"I believe in the pursuit of happiness, to be achieved by hard work at the office; by being friendly but sharp, shrewd, and aggressive. It includes playing it safe and cool on the market. I believe in the freedom to do whatever I want to do along as it doesn't hurt anyone else. I believe everyone has a right to economic security and a high standard of living to be gained by individual effort. I believe in staying busy and acquiring every gadget that makes life convenient. (Isn't it fun to shop until I drop?) I believe that almost all people are equal because they are alike in seeking pleasure and prestige. I believe it is better to be moving than still, better to be young than old, better to be comfortable than uncomfortable, better to be rich than poor, better to be liked than disliked. I believe in taking an occasional moral holiday, and having fun off the straight and narrow. Oh yes, and I believe in God, a kind Father of us all, who helps those who help themselves, and who blesses America and defends it against all evils, even the ones we prefer to tolerate; and in

Jesus, who taught us how to find happiness by being nice to each other; and in the church, one of the finest facilities we have in our community. Amen."

Could our largest moral problem today be that we live by two creeds, two sets of moral rules? One for our private selves and one for the world; one for in church on Sunday and one for the office during the rest of the week? Have we substituted the half-gods of happiness, status, and materialism for the Lord Himself?

The time has come for Christian and non-Christian alike to experience and extend the claim of Scripture – "Seek ye first the kingdom of God and His righteousness" – and other things will take their rightful place. What we do or don't do tells others what we really believe. A second look at ourselves will give authentic clues as to whom and whose we really are. Where we are or aren't on the Lord's Day is probably our first clue as to whether what we say or we believe is an accessory or ornament in our lives or the vital heartbeat in the living of our lives. Can God count on you and your family in worship this weekend and each week of your life?

Let The Church Go To Hell
Reflection/Quest Time

• **Exploring Questions for Discussion**
1. When considering your faith, how would you rate the balance of your beliefs and corresponding actions?
___ Miserable ___ Fair ___ Good ___ Admirable
2. Consider your worship record for the past two years and the ways in which you live your faith. What does this say to you? Can your faith unapplied survive?
3. Who or what truly guides your life choices? The teachings of Christ or the culture at large?

• **Related Scripture Sources**

Matthew 6:33   Matthew 9:22
Mark 12:34   Matthew 7:20-30
Romans 14:17-19   Colossians 3:1-4
Psalm 95:6-7

• **New Perspectives**
Consider personal changes you can make and/or new steps you can take to be of service to others.

• **Questions to be Resolved**
(Can be listed on a separate page)

• **A Prayer Thought**

"What shall we render unto the Lord for all His benefits to us?

We will walk before the Lord in the land of the living."

THE BATTLE OF
DECISION MAKING IN
CHARACTER DEVELOPMENT

There are those who have said, "I never liked history, but I loved those characters." As something of a Civil War buff, I am intrigued by this awesome American tragedy, knowing that it was also a defining moment in our national saga. Beyond reading books of the events and the personalities who shaped them, I find myself roaming battlefields, visiting museums, and attending Civil War Roundtables. Recently, I finished reading a new bestseller, *Gods and Generals*, a novel by Jeff Shaara featuring characterizations of four major military personalities of that great conflict. Shaara has put life into generals of the South and the North, namely, Lee, Jackson, Hancock, and Chamberlain.

One gets to know their thoughts and feelings in a shrewd depiction of character by examining the viewpoints and vulnerabilities of this fascinating collection of military minds. Robert E. Lee is portrayed as one who possesses an unwavering sense of dignity, but his dedication to duty and his care for those around him reveal him to be a man of extraordinary compassion and conscience. His faith is unquestioning. Winfield S. Hancock is depicted as a man possessing an annoying talent for the drudgery of army rules and paperwork. Stonewall Jackson has no vices and projects the qualities of being rigid and disciplined. He is known for a fiery religious conviction. Joshua L. Chamberlain is seen as brilliant with an amazing talent for mastering any subject. He considers the ministry as a career, but cannot make the final commitment. Throughout the book a picture is painted of each character as he might have understood his own world. Each decision they make centers on a question of loyalty and the principles of duty amid the horrors of their divided nation.

When we think of the Bible, we also see something dramatically more than an impersonal account of religious history. We find portraits of imperfect people engaged in journeys of faith that don't always end up in the paradise of success. The Bible is amazingly graphic in introducing us to characters who exhibit both character blemishes and virtues. The reader finds clues pointing to the transforming power of God in the midst of struggle and adversity.

A brief look at some key Biblical characters makes us aware that truth comes by way of personality and character. Two Old Testament leaders, Moses and Abraham, are identified through various snapshots of their inclinations. Moses is identified as "a man of God." (Deuteronomy 33:1), and in the book of Numbers, he is portrayed as inspiring. These qualities earmarked his leadership years in guiding the people of Israel. Abraham is described as a friend of God (Isaiah 41:8), and as possessing great personal piety (Genesis 12:7-8) and faith (Genesis 15:6). Not to be forgotten is his independence of character. God used each of these patriarchs as they exercised their gifts in performing God's call to service.

In the New Testament a captivating personality is Simon Peter. At times one wonders if he will make it as a disciple of Jesus. He is seen in a collage of impetuousness, boldness, and dependability ("the rock"), when he proclaims his confession of faith. Jesus, as the central reality of the New Testament, unfolds in notable life encounters as one who is moved with compassion for the multitudes and especially the marginalized. He weeps over the city of Jerusalem. Out of this character and mission, Jesus calls to each of us in the midst of our personal battlefields and beckons, "Come to Me, all you that are weary and are carrying heavy burdens, and I will give you rest. Take My yoke upon you, and learn from Me; for I am gentle and humble in heart, and you will find rest for your souls. For My yoke is easy, and My burden is light." (Matthew 11:28-30). This "man of sorrows," who is acquainted with grief and has engaged the battles of decision-making, gently urges us to follow Him.

THE BATTLE OF DECISION MAKING IN CHARACTER DEVELOPMENT
REFLECTION/QUEST TIME

• EXPLORING QUESTIONS FOR DISCUSSION
1. Decision making is an unavoidable process involving risk in one's life. Decisions are influenced by our character, and they also can contribute to the shape of our character. List some of the major decisions you have made which have been instrumental in your character development for better or worse.
2. What mistakes are commonly made when entertaining major life decisions?
3. Consider the qualities of decision making exhibited by some notable personalities of the Old and New Testament as listed in the scripture sources below (For example, Moses, Abraham, Simon Peter, and Jesus.). Identify their character traits.

• RELATED SCRIPTURE SOURCES

Deuteronomy 33:1	Numbers 14:12-20 (Moses)
Isaiah 4:1-8	Genesis 12:7-8
Genesis 15:6	Genesis 14:23; 23:6-16 (Abraham)

Matthew 4:18-20; 16:13-19 and other passages within the Gospels of Mark, Luke and John referring to Simon Peter.

Descriptions of Jesus' humanity, humility, and servanthood are found in Philippians 2:11. General references to Jesus' character and mission are found throughout the Gospels of Matthew, Mark, Luke, and John.

• NEW PERSPECTIVES
Consider personal changes you can make and/or new steps you can take to be of service to others.

• QUESTIONS TO BE RESOLVED
(Can be listed on a separate page)

• A Prayer Thought

"O Master, let me walk with You in lowly paths of service true;
Tell me your secret; help me bear the strain of toil, the fret of care.
Teach me Your patience; share with me a closer dearer company
in work that keeps faith sweet and strong, in trust that triumphs over
wrong, in hope that sends a shining ray far down the future's broad'ning
way, in peace that only You can give; with You, O Master, let me live."

Not For "Super Christians" Only

For baseball fans, these days are especially filled with drama and excitement as the World Series gradually reveals the champions of the sport. These are moments of great excitement for those whose favorite team wins and dull resignation for those whose team comes out second best.

One of the most poignant moments in the history of baseball was the final farewell of Lou Gehrig in Yankee Stadium. Suffering from an incurable disease, the great and revered first baseman stood at the plate and tearfully said farewell to the fans who had cheered him on for many years. Sooner or later, the time comes when each of us must "hang-up the spikes."

St. Paul's farewell speech is ranked by some interpreters as one of the great valedictory addresses of all times. In just a few words, he captured the essence of his whole life: "As for me, I am already being poured out as a libation, and the time of my departure has come. I have fought the good fight, I have finished the race, I have kept the faith. From now on there is reserved for me the crown of righteousness, which the Lord, the righteous judge, will give me on that day, and not only to me but also to all who have longed for His appearing." (2 Timothy 4:6-8)

Paul, the veteran missionary, had been loved and hated, supported and attacked, praised and cursed. Whatever else can be said of his life, it certainly wasn't dull. Anticipating the executioner's axe, he passed on the baton to his young friend Timothy, and entrusted to him the next lap of the race.

Life and ministry involve the daily working out of priorities. For each of us, there is more to do in a given day than can be done. There is much more we would like to do than can be done in a lifetime. Therefore, the establishing of clear priorities is a matter of extreme importance.

The metaphor Paul uses for his death ("the time of my departure") corresponds to the Greek work used for the loosening of ropes when taking down a tent. It is also used when describing the release of lines when a ship leaves the dock and for a sailor launching out on a new journey. Herein is the Christian view of death. Having given his best, Paul now sees himself as crossing the finish line.

The focus is not on winning as much as it is on finishing. One of our sons has run and finished the New York City Marathon. The other hopes to do so. Every marathon race has a winner but far more important to the dedicated marathon runner is completing the race. Christian life and ministry is not a competition to run better than others. It is a commitment to run all the way to the finish.

Finally, there is a reward. The crown of the Greek games was a laurel wreath awarded to the victor. In the case of our faith race, the crown goes not only to Paul but also "to all who have longed for [God's] appearing." Any thought that only "super Christians" get special awards is abolished. Such is Paul's view of both death and life – and all in 52 words. What a way to "hang up the spikes."

Not For "Super Christians" Only
Reflection/Quest Time

• **Exploring Questions for Discussion**

1. Life and ministry involve the daily working out of priorities. If this is a new day, what is the most important thing you will be doing? What is the most important thing you should be doing? What determines how you decide?

2. Is your faith designed for the long run and completing the race?

3. How might you build your endurance to finish the race of faith?

• **Related Scripture Sources**

2 Timothy 4:6-8   1 Corinthians 9:24-27
Hebrews 12:1-2

• **New Perspectives**

Consider personal changes you can make and/or new steps you can take to be of service to others.

• **Questions to be Resolved**

(Can be listed on a separate page)

• **A Prayer Thought**

"Lord, You give the great commission: "Heal the sick and preach the word."
Lest the Church neglect its mission and the Gospel go unheard,
Help us witness to Your purpose with renewed integrity:
With the Spirit's gifts empow'r us for the work of ministry.

Lord, You bless with words assuring: "I am with You to the end."
Faith and hope and love restoring, may we serve as You intend and,
Amid the cares that claim us, hold in mind eternity:
With the Spirit's gifts empow'r us for the work of ministry."

The Rainbow, a Sign of Hope and Promise in Troubled Times

We are told that the Lehigh Valley has had just twelve rainless days for many months. The weather for the most part has been dreary, cold, wet and sunless until recently. At last the clouds are beginning to welcome the sunshine. One of these days we are liable to see a rainbow.

Judy Garland sang in the movie The Wizard of Oz the nostalgic words and music of the song "Over the Rainbow." When I hear it sung it always causes me to whistle or sing those classic words:

"Somewhere over the rainbow, way up high; there's a land that I heard of once in a lullaby. Somewhere over the rainbow, skies are blue, and the dreams that you dare to dream really do come true.

Someday I'll wish upon a star and wake up where the clouds are far behind me. Where troubles melt like lemon drops, and way above the chimney tops, that's where you'll find me."

The refrain concludes with the question of "Why, oh why, can't I?"

But what about the clouds around us? There appears to be rising disillusionment among so many people young and old about the obvious signs of decay in morals, values, corruption in high places, and the prevailing lack of honesty, courtesy, and gruesome, inhuman crimes. Global unrest and the prevalence of crime are unsettling. Meaningless oaths and covenants of marriage are widespread, and they threaten the failure of our families forcing children to be given up as debris.

Our circumstances are similar to the time of Noah's generation described in the Bible. "The Lord saw that the wickedness of humankind was great in the earth, and that every inclination of the thoughts of their hearts were only evil continually." Scripture goes on to say that "the Lord was sorry that He had made mankind on the earth, and it grieved Him to His heart." (Genesis 6:5-6) God's judgment took the form of a destructive flood and God's mercy was shown in saving a remnant of a new historical beginning.

Noah, a righteous man, who was in right relationship with God, was chosen to build an ark at a time when "the earth was corrupt in God's sight" (Genesis 6:11) A worldwide deluge emerged and only Noah, his family, and the living creatures taken by him into the ark were saved from annihilation. When the deluge was over and dry land emerged, a rainbow appeared in the clouds to be a sign of God's covenant that "never again shall all flesh be cut off by the waters the waters of a flood." (Genesis 9:11) God promised to remember this at each appearance of a rainbow.

A couple of years ago, I was in Michigan for a speaking engagement in the middle of winter. The day I was scheduled to fly back to Bethlehem was preceded by a day of snow and sleet. The snowstorm continued as airports began one by one to cancel flights. My hosts volunteered to drive me to Saganaw, Michigan, where flights were still operative.

Realizing that I would need to catch a plane on odd schedules and destinations, I kept my suitcase with me. In this way, I could make quick exits for snap connections to the next destination in order to get home without getting stuck in some Midwest airport. I arrived home late at night after grabbing my suitcase at the front of the plane where mine was placed. I did not open it until the next morning, where I opened it on the floor of our large-sized bathroom. I realized rather quickly when I saw women's clothing and hair styling items that it wasn't my suitcase. As I stared at it intently, my wife walked into the room and said, "You are staring at that suitcase as if you think that if you stare at it long enough it will change." I began to notice in the midst of the clothing a little notebook which looked like a flight log with a woman's name. I realized that the suitcase probably belonged to a flight stewardess who had a suitcase identical to mine. In short order, I returned the case to the airport and in a few days my suitcase was delivered to our home. Two honest people had made a mistake. As a result, I've learned not to treat luggage so casually. Moreover, it was gratifying to experience mutual honesty.

A covenant of promise and obligation was fulfilled not by coercion or external command, but by a willing response found within the inclination of the human heart. The dreams that we dare to dream really can come true when we covenant to be bonded as partners with God seeking first the kingdom of God and His righteousness so as to have access to God's everlasting promise of love. Even in the midst of tragedy and current violence, one individual can faithfully walk with God. God's choice of imperfect Noah enables a glimmer of hope today in the midst of all that makes for decay and deterioration.

Narrow and self-centered vision is all around us. God's heart was filled with pain in Noah's sin-stained generation. God's heart was filled with pain when sinful man nailed Christ to the cross. And God's heart is filled with pain in our modern sin-filled world. God does not stand in an indifferent or remote relationship to what is happening but personally enters into our individual and global brokenness and works on it from within. The Savior seeks to enter our hearts and receive a willing response.

The closing lyrics of "Over the Rainbow" pose the question, "Why then, O why can't I?" The sign of God's promise is in the rainbow. His assurance is "I have set my bow in the clouds, and it shall be a sign of the covenant between me and the earth . . . I will remember My covenant that is between Me and you and every living creature of all flesh." (Genesis 9:13, 15) Jesus declares, "My sheep hear My voice. I know them, and they follow Me. I give them eternal life, and they will never perish. No one will snatch them out of My hand." (John 10:27-28) God adopted the rainbow and so can we. It is the sign of promise and hope in troubled times.

The Rainbow, a Sign of Hope and Promise in Troubled Times
Reflection/Quest Time

• **Exploring Questions for Discussion**
1. God promises to remember His covenant with each of us. What does this suggest about the character of God, especially in troubled times?
2. What part have you played in offering a willing response to nurture a covenantal relationship with God's promise?
3. Can you rightfully claim that God has first place in your life?

• **Related Scripture Sources**

Genesis 6:5, 6, 11   Genesis 9:8-17 John 10:27-28

• **New Perspectives**
Consider personal changes you can make and/or new steps you can take to be of service to others.

• **Questions to be Resolved**
(Can be listed on a separate page)

• **A Prayer Thought**

"Praise to You, O Lord,
We render for Your love in Jesus shown;
May that love, so strong and tender,
Bind us fast to Him alone;
Now and ever, now and ever,
Gather us among Your own."

Billboards Can Remind Us of Important Truths

Maybe you've seen the highway billboard: It reads, "What part of the 'You Shall Not . . .' didn't you understand?" and it is signed "God."

I like it. It gets to the heart of things. Will it be God or gods who control and guide your life?

Some years ago, on the cover of the Saturday Evening Post, there was a painting by Norman Rockwell of a woman buying her Thanksgiving turkey. The turkey is on the scales and the butcher is standing behind the counter, apron pulled tight over his fat stomach, a pencil tucked behind his ear. The customer, a lovely lady of about 60, is watching the weighing-in. Each has a pleased look as if each knows a secret joke.

Rockwell lets us in on the joke. The butcher is pushing on the scale with a big fat thumb. The woman is pushing up on it with a dainty forefinger. Neither is aware of what the other is doing. Both would resent being called thieves, but neither saw anything wrong with a little deception that would make a few cents for one or save a few cents for the other.

Rockwell gives us a picture of how we seek to live, trying to manipulate life to our advantage. And that's what the Ten Commandments are all about. They remind us that there are eternal laws by which we must live if life is going to come out God's way.

No document has influenced Western culture to the degree that the Ten Commandments has. For Jews and Christians, this represents a formulation of the religious principles held in common. The first four commandments address our relationship to God, while the next six address our relationship to others. To hear what God has to say, we begin with the One who initiates the Covenant: "I am the Lord your God who brought you out of the land of Egypt, out of the house of bondage." Though we do not list this as one of the Ten Commandments, there is a sense in which a commandment is implicit. We are to know and acknowledge God as the One who has delivered us, and as the first word of the Bible says, as the One who created us.

So the commandment is "Know Me! Acknowledge Me! Remember Me! I am the Lord your God. The first commandment is stated in the word, "You shall love the Lord your God with all your heart, and with all your soul, and with all your might." (Deuteronomy 6:5)

The rest of the commandments mean little or nothing unless commitment to God comes first. It is not uncommon, however, for financial security, power, social prestige, love of country, love of family, profession or job to replace God as our first commitment.

God is a personal God, available to our needs. The Scripture is filled with that witness. "I called to the Lord out of my distress, and He answered me." (Jonah 2:2) "And my God will fully satisfy every need of yours according to His riches in glory in Christ Jesus." (Philippians 4:19) "Even though I walk through the darkest valley, I fear no evil; for You are with me; Your rod and Your staff – they comfort me." (Psalms 23:4). The question is not whether we believe in a god, but whether we believe in God, worship God, and commit ourselves to God without reservation.

I believe that theologian Elton Trueblood was correct when he stated that to take the name of the Lord in vain is a commandment warning against taking God lightly. We break this and the other commandments when we say we believe in God and that we accept the ideals of His kingdom, but we don't take Him seriously. This is a form of atheism.

We're atheists in practice, though we may call ourselves Christian, Jewish or Muslim. We're atheists when we live much of our lives as though God does not matter. Take a few minutes to consider these questions:
• What do I think about most when I'm not thinking about my work?
• How do I spend my leisure time?
• How do I spend my money?
My hunch is that our answers will provide some shocking revelations. Probably most of us will discover we spend much more time watching television than reading the Bible, in prayer, or worship. In addition, we spend most of our leisure time and money on amusing ourselves rather than helping others.

Maybe it's time to return to the original question.

"What part of 'You Shall Not . . .' didn't you understand?"

Billboards Can Remind Us of Important Truths
Reflection/Quest Time

- **Exploring Questions for Discussion**
1. Are you aware of some minor gods who have essentially replaced God in your life?
2. Have there been times in your life when you have acted as a spiritual atheist because you have not taken God seriously?

- **Related Scripture Sources**

Deuteronomy 6:5	Psalms 23:4
Jonah 2:2	Philippians 4:17

- **New Perspectives**
Consider personal changes you can make and/or new steps you can take to be of service to others.

- **Questions to be Resolved**
(Can be listed on a separate page)

- **A Prayer Thought**
"Jesus leads us onward in the high mission of the church. We proclaim the Gospel to all nations by word and deed, that people everywhere may find new life in God. We hear You call. We pledge the best of our labors, that Your glory may be known in all the earth."

In Search
of God

It seems rather human to be in search of something regardless of our age or circumstances. Our searches take us in all directions. The efforts range from the simple to the bizarre.

Our country was seeking a savior in its search for a president among the candidates. Millions of dollars have been spent to put the most attractive spin on the candidates to influence our vote.

Something of the search is heralded by the weekly ISO sections in newspapers. This, I learned, stands for men and women "in search of" a companion, relationship, marriage or fling. People advertise themselves seeking to attract the right person to satisfy their search.

Their goals differ widely. One woman described her search this way: "Abiding, striking, vivacious woman loves films, football, dancing, kisses. Seeks man who is generous, brilliant, lean, well-dressed, and vigorous soul mate/partner."

Another searcher with a touch of creativity suggested, "All the right stuff: attractive, fit, accomplished, tall, courageous, in search of a permanent co-pilot, to fly me to the moon." Here's hoping.

Men were equally creative in their search of female friendships or courting, or more. One man described himself as a "Lonely Pooh Bear looking for a woman to snuggle with."

Another male, more explicit, identified his search saying, "Sexy, cool male, 30, tall, toned, secure, seeks sexy, cool, dark-eyed woman, 30-36, physically, emotionally fit for Sinatra, champagne, and intrigue."

The search goes on. One can only wonder how many sincere or flamboyant persons have their dreams come true as a result of their ISO advertisements.

Can any of us get below the surface of our self-centered searching in order to discover our hidden hunger and the real gifts that only God can provide?

Jesus seemed to stimulate this awareness in his Sermon on the Mount as He emphasized, "Blessed are those who hunger and thirst for righteousness, for they will be filled." (Matthew 5:6)

He focused on the real searching that brings satisfaction by insisting, "But strive first for the kingdom of God and His righteousness, and all these things will be given to you as well." (Matthew 6:33) Our goals must be kept in sight, lest we let the good interfere with the best in our life journey.

Something of this sight in our search for achieving rightful goals is told in the account of Florence Chadwick who became the first woman to swim Catalina Channel, eclipsing the men's record by two hours. When she looked ahead, Chadwick saw nothing but a solid wall of fog and her body was numb. She had been swimming for nearly 16 hours.

Already she was the first woman to swim the English Channel in both directions. Now, at age 34, her goal was to become the first woman to swim from Catalina Island to the California coast.

On that Fourth of July morning in 1952, the sea was like an ice bath and the fog was so dense she could hardly see her support boats. Sharks cruised toward her lone figure, only to be driven away by rifle shots. Against the frigid grip of the sea, she struggled on – hour after hour – while millions watched on national television.

Alongside Florence, in one of the boats, her mother and her trainer offered encouragement. They told her it wasn't much farther. But all she could see was fog. They urged her not to quit. She never had – until then. With only a half-mile to go, she asked to be pulled out.

Still thawing her chilled body several hours later, she told a reporter, "Look, I'm not excusing myself, but if I could have seen land I might have made it."

It was not fatigue or even the cold water that defeated her. It was the fog. She was unable to see her goal.

Two months later, she tried again. This time, despite the same dense fog, she swam with her faith intact and her goal clearly pictured in her mind. She knew that somewhere behind that fog was land and this time she made it.

What is your goal? What are you in search of? Why not get real about it and enable yourself to see the goal. Is the goal to seek first the kingdom of God and His righteousness reflected in your chosen way of life?

IN SEARCH OF GOD
REFLECTION/QUEST TIME

• RELATED SCRIPTURE SOURCES

Matthew 5:6	1 Peter 5:5-11
Matthew 6:11-34	1 Thessalonians 4:1-8
Romans 12:1-3, 12:9-18	

• NEW PERSPECTIVES

Consider personal changes you can make and/or new steps you can take to be of service to others.

• QUESTIONS TO BE RESOLVED

(Can be listed on a separate page)

• A PRAYER THOUGHT

"We confess, Lord, that as Your disciples we have often dishonored the
    holy name we bear.
We ask Your forgiveness for the times when we have failed to labor for
    Your kingdom;
When we have not followed Your admonition to seek first the kingdom
    of God;
When we have hidden our light from the world;
When we, as the salt of the earth, have lost our strength.
Have mercy on us, and restore unto us the joy of faithful discipleship.

The Lord, your Redeemer, has said: With everlasting love, I will have
compassion on you. Therefore, serve the Lord with gladness; witness to His
goodness and mercy, and present Jesus Christ as Lord, with yourselves as
servants for Jesus sake."

Somewhere To Be

We had some important decisions to make recently when becoming residents of a local retirement community consisting of single floor apartments. As we prepared to move, my wife and I pondered, for example, what to do with our beloved St. Francis. He is our wood-carved, man-sized monk figure who now stands looking over the garden in the rear of our new home. It is a natural place for him, as one who showed his love to animals, birds, plants, people, and even the inanimate natural world.

By now, our St. Francis statue is rather well known to residents and guests of the community who have walked by and stopped to look him over, to talk to him, to stand in silent vigil, to place family and grandchildren with him for photos, or to use him as a frame of reference for guiding incoming guests. He is important to many, even though he is in a rather remote spot at the end of our lawn.

"Somewhere to be" – these are the words used by a young student with whom I have recently formed a close relationship. One day, as we were sitting in the college cafeteria, he told me of his difficulties, including the anxiety that never left him and often times turned to panic and to flight. He was trying to look objectively at what was going on inside of himself and to understand it. Then, as if summing up his thoughts, he looked up to me and said: "Basically, I'm always looking for a place – for somewhere to be." Sometimes a remark unexpectedly strikes an answering note in our hearts and minds. This student's remark appears to be one of the fundamental needs of all men and women, and the distress that besets a large number of them.

For many of us there are favorite places to be – a favorite view, a reflection in a lake, a street corner, a tree, a fountain, or a favorite pew in church. Such places are remembered by some as the scene of a decisive experience of both human and divine fellowship. One hymn says it so well, "There is a place of quiet rest, near to the heart of God." This is a place for you and me.

Perhaps the famous words of St. Francis are helpful in finding our place to be in the world:

Lord, make me an instrument of your peace
Where there is hatred, let me sow love,
Where there is injury, pardon;
Where there is doubt, faith;
Where there is despair, hope;

Where there is darkness, light;
Where there is sadness, joy.
O divine Master, grant that I may not so much week
To be consoled, as to console,
To be understood, as to understand,
To be loved, as to love,
For it is in giving that we receive.
It is in pardoning that we are pardoned;
It is in dying that we are born to eternal life.

SOMEWHERE TO BE
REFLECTION/QUEST TIME

• EXPLORING QUESTIONS FOR DISCUSSION
1. Where do you long to be?
2. What prevents you from finding that place in your heart?
3. What steps can you take now to find a place where you will be at peace?

• RELATED SCRIPTURE SOURCES
John 14:18-31   John 14:1-6
John 8:30-39   Ephesians 1:3

• NEW PERSPECTIVES
Consider personal changes you can make and/or new steps you can take to be of service to others.

• QUESTIONS TO BE RESOLVED
(Can be listed on a separate page)

• A PRAYER THOUGHT

"There is a place of quiet rest, near to the heart of God,
A place where sin cannot molest,
Near to the heart of God.

There is a place of comfort sweet, near to the heart of God,
A place where we our Savior meet,
Near to the heart of God.

There is a place of full release, near to the heart of God,
A place where all is joy and peace, near to the heart of God."

PAGE 35, HYMNS FOR THE FAMILY OF GOD

What Does It Mean
to be Lost?

A speaker at a well known Tabernacle in the popular summer resort town of Ocean City, New Jersey, tells of his experience in his hotel room overlooking the Atlantic Ocean and the busy boardwalk which parallels the seaside. Thousands of people stroll or ride bicycles along the boardwalk and frequent the famous saltwater taffy shops or the amusement parks situated along the way.

From his room he could see the endless streams of people walking aimlessly. A blend of clattering voices and the carnival sounds of the merry-go-round floated into his room on the soft, salty, humid summer night's breeze. And then came an anonymous announcement over the public address system stating, "A little girl about five years of age, answering to the name of Wendy, has been lost. She is wearing a yellow dress and carrying a teddy bear. She has brown eyes, auburn hair. Anyone knowing the whereabouts of Wendy, please report to the Music Pier. Her parents are waiting for her there."

In hearing this announcement, one can only wonder about Wendy. Where was she in what must have looked to be a forest of legs along the Boardwalk? How did she feel without the clasp of her father's strong hand? One can imagine Wendy clutching her faithful teddy bear, tears streaming down her face, her heart bursting with fright and loneliness.

Picture her parents. That triggered my own parental concerns and flooded me with memories of times my own children have gotten lost. What must they be feeling? Imagine all the tragic things that could happen to Wendy: the sea, physical harm, strangers . . .

Wendy was found, the speaker finally noted. I could picture the thankful looks of love on her parents' faces and feel the joy they must have expressed. I can hear something inside me saying, "It's alright now, Wendy. Don't cry anymore. It's okay. We've found you. Never let go of my hand again. I love you Wendy."

In a further look at the streams of humanity along the boardwalk we might ask, how many of them were lost and didn't know it? Or how many felt a deep sense inside of being lost and wished an announcement would be made about their spiritual condition? How many more didn't even care? I wonder how many of them knew that they needed a heavenly Father as much as Wendy needed her daddy?

The parables of the lost sheep and the lost coin (Luke 15:1-10) immediately come to mind. These parables communicate with undeniable vividness that God is concerned about the lost, cares about individuals, and is consumed with an active, seeking love for you and me. What kind of a shepherd would leave 99 sheep in an open pasture to search for one gone astray? Why was one so important?

What does it mean to be lost? Some who read this can feel the sense of being lost that I describe; they have no intimate relationship with God. Others of us are lost in a different way; we no longer desire the Shepherd to guide our lives. Still others of us have lost our direction; we feel lost in the multiplicity of alternatives. There is also the lost feeling associated with the recognition that one has failed God, and needs forgiveness and a new beginning.

The drama of the parable found in Luke 15 has four acts, each built around key words: the word "lost" describes our condition; "go after" portrays God's searching love; "He finds" reveals the persistence of His grace, and "joy" dramatizes the Lord's response to finding us.

Maybe the prophet's word is a needy reminder, "All we like sheep have gone astray." (Isaiah 53:6) There is joy for any one of us who desperately need to know that the Shepherd has found us.

What Does It Mean to be Lost?
Reflection/Quest Time

• Exploring Questions for Discussion

1. Consider a few instances when you were lost. What caused you to become lost? How did you react? How did you eventually find your way?

2. Can you give an example of a person you know who you believe has lost his/her way in life? What has led you to this conclusion? What can you learn from his/her mistakes? Is there anything you can do to help him/her?

3. The parable of the lost sheep and the lost coin (Luke 15:1-10) convey God's concern for the lost, and His desire to discover the lost. Are you ready to be found?

• Related Scripture Sources

Luke 15:1-10   Matthew 18:10-12
Isaiah 53:16

• New Perspectives

Consider personal changes you can make and/or new steps you can take to be of service to others.

• Questions to be Resolved

(Can be listed on a separate page)

• A Prayer Thought

"God of certainty, God of truth, our confidence is in You and in You alone. Yet we live in a fallen world and we are an imperfect people. Our world is filled with pain and alienation. We know of illness when body or mind is failing, and the loneliness of spirit it brings. We know of separation from parent or child, from friend or neighbor, and the emptiness of life it brings. We know of strangeness in new communities and in changing communities, and the longing it brings. We know of alienation caused by unemployment or poverty or discrimination, and the pain it brings. We have become strangers to our relatives and foreigners to our families.

How can we sing the Lord's song in a strange land? Let our cry for help come to You. I am a God nearby, says the Lord. Do I not fill heaven and earth? I am the Lord your God. I have called you out from the peoples and you shall be holy to Me."

JUDGING OTHERS
BY FIRST IMPRESSIONS

Have you noticed that people – including you and me – are prone to see other people's weaknesses first, before we get to know them and discover their strengths and good points? Some years ago, I received a fresh reminder on this human tendency to latch on to the negative impressions of others, before we emphasize the worth and value of our fellow travelers in life.

During the 1960s, I was pursuing a Ph.D. at Temple University's Graduate School of Religion. For a number of years, I traveled once a week from Ohio for a day of classes in Philadelphia.

The first year I traveled with another student, and we drove in an old station wagon to engage in nine hours of class studies. The driver lived in a small neighboring town and drove us all night, and slept part of the next day before he participated in some sales activity the other part of the day.

One day, we didn't have the necessary parking tokens for the university parking lot. So the driver parked on a side street to await our purchase of tokens when the school office opened up. While he waited in the car, he fell asleep. Two coeds from a nearby dorm came out of their front door and observed our crummy car.

Next to our driver on the front seat was a plastic toy machine gun, which he brought along to return to one of my sons who had been given the gun as a gift following recent surgery.

Upon seeing the gun and our driver slumped in the front seat, the students notified campus security about the strange car with sleeping bags in the rear and what looked like a gun in the front. Since this was a time when race riots marred the peace of the city, the campus police sensed that this was a situation too big for them.

They called in the city police under the command of Frank Rizzo, then police commissioner, who was well known for his riot squads who raced to trouble spots in large brown riot buses loaded with police equipped with riot clubs, guns, and tear gas.

In a matter of minutes, they had closed off the streets with police cars and surrounded our unsuspecting driver and station wagon with club-bearing officers. They jerked out driver from the car as he pleaded that he could explain the circumstances. They placed him against the car and upturned the inside of the car until they found the toy machine gun.

In disgust and with unprintable words, they told our driver to hide the gun and never to return to Pennsylvania with it or any other suspicious weapons.

Our driver ran into the university office to find my partner and me.

"You'll never believe it," he yelled before explaining what happened. Then he sought a place of refuge where he could sleep unnoticed for the rest of the day. Upon my return to Ohio, I preached on Family Sunday and used the Philadelphia incident as an illustration.

I commented that the students and police saw the gun, and neglected to notice my Bible and other textbooks alongside the gun. I added that this traumatic experience was very similar to our inclinations in classifying strangers or new acquaintances. We judge negatively on the outside to the neglect of evaluating the positive on the inside.

Jesus suggested this possibility when he said that man judges on the outside but God looks upon the heart on the inside. Consider not judging others by first impressions, and take the time to let God's love of each guide us to the good of others on the inside. Try it! It works!

Judging Others by First Impressions
Reflection/Quest Time

• Exploring Questions for Discussion

1. Is it natural for us to judge others? If yes, why do you think that we do this?

2. What for us are the implications of the Lord's statement to Samuel that "the Lord does not see as mortals see; they look on the outward appearance, but Lord looks on the heart?"

• Related Scripture Sources

1 Samuel 16:7-12	Psalm 11:7-9
2 Corinthians 10:7	Jeremiah 10:10
John 7:24	2 Corinthians 5:12-16

• New Perspectives

Consider personal changes you can make and/or new steps you can take to be of service to others.

• Questions to be Resolved

(Can be listed on a separate page)

• A Prayer Thought

"Is not this the kind of worship that pleases men, says our God; to undo the bonds of injustice, to let the oppressed go free and break every yoke, to share bread with the hungry and shelter the homeless poor, to clothe the naked and not turn from your own people? I was hungry and you fed Me, thirsty and you gave Me drink, a stranger and you welcomed Me, naked and you clothed Me, sick or in prison and you visited Me.

When did we see You hungry and feed You, thirsty and give You drink? When did we see You a stranger and welcome You, naked and clothe You, sick or in prison and visit You?

Truly, I say to you, when you did it to one of the least of these, you did it to Me."

RIPPLES OF GOD'S
RIVERS OF LIFE

Rivers have always been fascinating to me. Two in particular have become rather personal over recent months – the Little Laramie in Wyoming and the Big Blackfoot in Montana. We went ranching in Wyoming one September in an Elderhostel program. Wyoming's face has been sculptured by the forces of geology – wind, water, fire ice – into a grand playground of rolling plains, landscape-carving rivers, prairies, lakes, and continent-dividing mountains. Wyoming is the mother of great rivers – the Snake, the Green, the Wind/Big Horn, the Powder, and the Yellowstone.

On the ranch where we stayed, the Little Laramie River flowed in front of our cabin. Each day fresh fish were caught in its entrancing waters. Our horseback rides took us through the river. We never lost our awareness that the ranch revolved around the river.

Over the years, most of us have had our eyes transfixed on the ravages of the mighty Mississippi River. Torrential and persistent rains have produced their natural consequences. Massive flooding has swarmed over the river banks along with the manmade limitations and encroachments. The river has claimed its territory. Devastation and the attending miseries are stupendous.

"Old Man River" is known for centuries for its flow and its floods, its fertilization of the lowlands, its challenge to the early pioneers going westward, its lore to the sentimental, the artistic and the musical, its usage for commerce, as well as the leisurely who bask as they float up and down this impressive river on the decks of river boats as the legendary "Delta Queen." Even I have been adventuresome in ice fishing on the Minnesota headwaters of the Mississippi.

I have been captivated by the theme "A River Runs Through It" which is made famous by the beautiful movie and book by that title. I have seen the movie and read the book twice, each time entranced and deeply moved by the beauty and the message. The story involves a father, his two sons, and the Big Blackfoot River near Missouri, Montana. The father and two sons are frequently and magnetically drawn to the sounds of the Big Blackfoot River with their soul and memories, and a four-count rhythm of fly fisherman, and the hope that a fish will rise.

They portray a river which has so many things to say that it is hard to know what it says to each of us, and their story ends much like Jesus' parable of the Prodigal Son. The younger son strays into gambling, a promiscuous lifestyle, and ultimately a violent death. And the waiting, loving father, in his ascending years, is buoyed up by his fond memories of the fishing experiences along the river with his sons and the elegant skills of his youngest but deceased son.

The Bible is chuck-full of references to rivers and waters. Rivers are mentioned in a figurative sense to reflect such things as prosperity (Isaiah 66:12), righteousness (Amos 5:24), and God's blessing to a "river of the water of life." (Revelation 22:1) In describing the "new" Jerusalem coming down out of heaven from God, the glory of God is portrayed like a radiance of a "very rare jewel, like jasper, clear as crystal." And in the midst of this new city is "the river of life, bright as crystal, flowing from the throne of God and the Lamb through the middle of the street of the city." "On either side of the river is the tree of life . . . and the leaves of the tree are for the healing of the nations. Nothing accursed will be found there anymore. But the throne of God and of the Lamb will be in it, and His servants will worship Him; they will see His face and His name will be on their foreheads." (Revelation 22:1-5)

A river runs through it all - perennial stream of righteousness and a source of God's blessing. Flowing from the heart of God is His truth, His love, and His righteousness. As for the heavenly vision expressed here on earth, the river of life runs through the center of our cities, into our sanctuaries, and hopefully into our lives for the healing of the nations. We are called and challenged to worship God in spirit and in truth.

We all need healing. But we are all prone likewise to have our defenses, our alibis, our attitudes, our sins, and our self-centered fortifications which block the flow of God's love. We end up limiting the Lord's healing power. God can make the valley green again. His eternal purpose is to bring life new and steady. This is what Jesus sought to communicate to you and me. (John 10:10) Perhaps this is our time to hear the message, "let My 'river of life' run through your life." Get ready for the blessing.

Ripples of God's Rivers of Life
Reflection/Quest Time

• **Exploring Questions for Discussion**
1. Do you have memories of a favorite river or body of water? What life truths did it teach you?
2. What other aspects of the heavenly vision portrayed in Revelation 22:1-5 enrich our understandings here on earth?
3. In what ways does the "river of life" run through your life? Give some specific examples.

• **Related Scripture Sources**

Isaiah 65:12   Revelation 22:1-5
Amos 5:24   John 10:10

• **New Perspectives**
Consider personal changes you can make and/or new steps you can take to be of service to others.

• **Questions to be Resolved**
(Can be listed on a separate page)

• **A Prayer Thought**

"They shall hunger no more, neither thirst anymore; the sun shall not strike them, nor any scorching heat; for the Lamb at the center of the throne will be their shepherd, and will guide them to springs of living water.

And God shall wipe away every tear from their eyes.

Almighty God, Redeemer and Sustainer, we offer You thanks and praise for the holy lives of all Your servants – the prophets, apostles, and martyrs – who have shown forth as lights in the world and sacrificed their lives in testimony of their faith."

IS REAL PEACE STILL WELL WITHIN REACH?

Directly or indirectly, all of us have been hit internally by the recent terror attacks in America. Shadows of thought and deep reflection surround the huge volume of questions which haunt us personally, in the nation, and around the world, as shock, misery, grief, and death mount in a thousand different directions. Our deepest wish is to "get back to normal."

Last December, our extended family of children and grandchildren spent two days in New York City. While we were there, we stayed at a hotel just across the street from the Twin Towers. The twinkle of holiday lights and the massive skyscape of the towers were fully visible from our windows.

These sights and the hotel are gone forever. On the other side of the hotel stood St. Paul's Church, which remains unscathed – without as much of a broken window.

We ponder and cherish our time and experiences together as a family, as we revisit in memories that setting. Beyond the nostalgia and past joys also looms the question, "What happened?" The full reality is still unfinished but a few observations surface.

We are never fully aware that our thinking has not caught up with technology. The fact is that technology has advanced beyond the point of capable defenses. We also realize that some of the greatest dangers to the world can come from a single, diabolical human being living in an unknown location. There is no guaranteed safety anywhere, for anyone.

If we confront these diabolical potentials openly and honestly, we probably will need more than a glass of warm milk to sleep at night. But, we are left asking, can we sincerely pray for the salvation of people while at the same time we are arming to kill others?

The old competitive nationalism, with its seeds of the destruction of humankind, must be challenged by every person of faith. Above all, the real source of peace is still within our reach and the foundation of all reality.

Some choice reminders of scripture are a basic source of faith and renewal. Hear them again:

"And he said to the woman, "Your faith has saved you, go in peace." (Luke 7:50)

"Peace I leave with you, my peace I give to you. I do not give to you as the world gives. Do not let your hearts be troubled, and do not let them be afraid." (John 14:27)

"I have said this to you, so that in Me you may have peace. In the world you face persecution. But take courage; I have conquered the world!" (John 16:33)

"Therefore, since we are justified by faith, we have peace with God through our Lord Jesus Christ." (Romans 5:1)

"Let us then pursue what makes for peace and for mutual upbuilding." (Romans 14:19)

"May the God of hope fill you with all joy and peace in believing, so that you may abound in hope by the power of the Holy Spirit." (Romans 15:13)

In the midst of the confusion Jesus whispers, "Peace."

Is Real Peace Still Well Within Reach?

Reflection/Quest Time

• Exploring Questions for Discussion

1. What has it meant for your life to recognize that there is no guaranteed safety anywhere for anyone?
2. Can we pray with sincerity for the salvation of people, while at the same time we are arming to kill others?
3. Define and describe peace on the basis of the scriptures cited in the article.

• Related Scripture Sources

Luke 7:50   John 14:27
Romans 8:6   Romans 14:19
Romans 15:13   John 16:33

• New Perspectives

Consider personal changes you can make and/or new steps you can take to be of service to others.

• Questions to be Resolved

(Can be listed on a separate page)

• A Prayer Thought

"If you do away with the yoke, the clenched fist, the wicked word; if you give your bread to the hungry and relief to the oppressed, then your light will rise like the dawn; your goodness will go before you and the glory of God behind you.

God has shown us what is good and what is required: to do justice, to show constant love, and to walk humbly with our God.

As we consider these things, let us confess our sins in silence.

The peace of Christ be with you;

And also with you."

THE TIE THAT BINDS
OUR HEARTS

What excites you? What depresses you? The human condition gives most of us a good dose of both, especially in these times which seem to be incredibly creative while destructively cruel.

For my wife and me, a gentleman we call "Luke of Prague" has been a source of excitement in these recent months. He has reentered our lives after meeting and being befriended by him in Prague over twenty-five years ago, during our travels and visits behind the Iron Curtain: in Russia, East Germany, Poland, Hungary, and Czechoslovakia. Luke – a young engineer – personally took us on a tour of Moravian churches throughout Czechoslovakia. We experienced an awesome reception of hospitality by pastors and laypeople, unrivaled by anything we have ever encountered anywhere in our lifetime. Luke chose to identify with us and to share his kinship, at a time when it could have cost him his future in education and employment.

Suddenly, this past fall, Luke reentered our lives by making contact from the University of Toronto where he is a Senior Research Fellow at the Institute of Micro-molecular Chemistry at the Academy of Sciences. Since then, my wife and I have visited with him at the New Dawn Moravian Church in Toronto. Now we are expecting a visit by Luke and his wife here in Bethlehem, if he can extend his visa.

Back in 1971, Luke's warmth and receptivity came in stark contrast to our experience in Russia, where we were separated from our tour group and incarcerated for forty-eight hours because of the lack of a visa within our passports. All other tour group members had their visas. In the process of detention, we were placed on the seventh floor of a building in Moscow, behind locked doors and under twenty-four hour surveillance. Without food for the first twenty-four hours and in total separation from our guide and group, we felt the eeriness that comes with unpredictable circumstances.

We were aware of others who disappeared completely under similar circumstances, and we clung to our devotional, the Moravian Daily Text. On that day, we remember reading the message of the psalmist, "Often have they attacked me from my youth, yet they have not prevailed against me." (Psalm 129:2)

A simple hymn verse accompanied the Scripture:
    He who is by Christ directed,
    Trusting the Good Shepherd's care,
    From all harm will be protected,
    And no danger needs to fear.

The prayer for the day stated:

Monday again . . . is that all there is to being a Christian . . .
Sunday morning church and afternoon picnic?
Guide and keep me by Your name,
that I might truly be the name You have given me – Christian.

The second twenty-four hours of incarceration in another location was equally confusing and depressing, but again we returned to the scriptural watchword of the Daily Text, where the words from the Old Testament commendation in Joshua declares, "Be strong and courageous; do not be frightened or dismayed, for the Lord your God is with you wherever you go." (Joshua 1:9) A New Testament text for the same day added to a sense of growing confidence for this special pilgrimage. This word was from the Book of Hebrews, ". . . Let us run with perseverance the race that is set before us, looking to Jesus the pioneer and perfecter of our faith . . ." (Hebrews 12:2)

At the end of the second day, we were permitted to rejoin our group and continue our stay in Russia and visit the other countries. Our remaining stay in the Soviet Union was very friendly and uplifting.

The visit with Luke in Czechoslovakia ended with a dramatic conclusion, when I placed a monetary gift in an envelope to cover the expenses incurred and tried to give it to him. In spite of his very limited financial circumstances, he refused the gift saying, "I am not a taxi. I am your brother." His words were the gift of a lifetime. His kinship in companionship and faith has endured over these years. We get excited as we experience the reality of "the tie that binds our hearts in Christian love." (Hymn: "Bless Be the Tie That Binds.")

These days are perplexing for all people of goodwill. Our century has compounded the destructive forces of fear, brutality, death, frustration, and depression. But each of us has a personal investment in being true and constant where we live – at work or love. In the midst of the darkest night or the most trying circumstances, there is something more for us to be and to do.

THE TIE THAT BINDS OUR HEARTS
REFLECTION/QUEST TIME

• EXPLORING QUESTIONS FOR DISCUSSION

1. Is that all there is to being a person of faith . . . Sunday morning church and afternoon picnic . . .?

2. What qualities, attitudes, or actions constitute "the tie that binds our hearts in Christian love"?

3. What kind of daily devotional guide do you use to nurture your faith?

• RELATED SCRIPTURE SOURCES

    Psalm 129:2   Joshua 1:9

    Hebrews 12:2-3

• NEW PERSPECTIVES

Consider personal changes you can make and/or new steps you can take to be of service to others.

• QUESTIONS TO BE RESOLVED

(Can be listed on a separate page)

• A PRAYER THOUGHT

"God of mercy, God of comfort, we come before You in this time of difficulty, mindful of human frailty and need, confused and struggling to find meaning in the face of suffering.

We are grateful that even as we share in the joy of Christ Jesus, we can also share abundantly in comfort in the midst of suffering."

CAN SURPRISES LEAD TO RENEWAL?

Bloopers are familiar to all of us. We've all committed a blooper or heard or read one. Recently, I read some bulletin bloopers in various churches. Here are two of my favorites:

At the evening service tonight, the sermon topic will be "What is Hell?" Come early and listen to our choir practice.

The eighth graders will be presenting Shakespeare's "Hamlet" in the church basement noon Friday at 7 p.m. The congregation is invited to attend this tragedy.

Embarrassing errors or unexpected turns of events can stimulate a good laugh or mar our existence. Here's an example of the former:

The story is told of a man who won a million dollars in the state lottery. He won the lottery while in critical condition in a hospital's intensive care unit after a heart attack. As a church member, he was not known for his generosity. As a matter of fact, he had the reputation of being stingy. His wife and daughter debated how to inform him of his fortune, without shocking him and hurting his recovery. They decided to ask their pastor to break the news in a thoughtful way.

The pastor hesitantly agreed, but chose his words carefully. When he got to the hospital room there were all those tubes, and lights, and signals, and oxygen connected up to the man. At what he deemed the right moment the pastor asked, "John if you were to win a million dollars, what would you do with it?"

After a moment the man replied, "I'd give it to the church"

The pastor died.

Unexpected surprises can be positive or negative depending on our readiness to respond. This is a season to reflect and renew. The Epistle lesson to be read during Lent is found in Ephesians 5:1-21. This passage amounts to advice by the apostle Paul on the nature of the Christian walk to a group of former pagans. It comes with three emphases: 1) Live in Love; 2) Live as Children of Light; and 3) Live in Wisdom.

These themes came at a special time in these new converts' experience and in what in history was known as "evil times." Some of these evils are identified as fornication, covetousness, filthiness, idolatry and foolish jesting – all of which sound very similar to our experience today.

As children of God, we are to imitate God within our individual life spheres, just as God is present in His universe, and thus prove that God is our Father. In further description of the Christian walk, St. Paul exhorts us to "live as children of the light," and he encourages believers to discover what is pleasing to the Lord. Living as children of light, a new walk with the Lord partakes of the highest elements of God's radiance that will manifest itself in our conduct. One can move from darkness to light, and begin to live a new vision.

The Christian walks in love, in light, and in wisdom. This is the ultimate for which all persons and civilized societies are to strive. Practical wisdom makes conduct consistent with faith. The debasement of society can never be an excuse for relaxing our witness or acquiescing to lower moral standards. We are facing more than a blooper or single shocking experience. We are engaged in spiritual warfare. It is a continual battle within our souls and among the souls of mankind. The aim is to mimic God's life in the world – to imitate Him in His outpouring of love, forgiveness, and sacrificial service.

CAN SURPRISES LEAD TO RENEWAL?
REFLECTION/QUEST TIME

• **EXPLORING QUESTIONS FOR DISCUSSION**

1. Is living in "evil times" motivation for surrender and withdrawal, or for renewal, commitment, and earnestness in our walk of faith, devotion, and action? Cite some examples of the two alternatives.

2. Consider some surprises which have led to renewal in your life. Portray these surprises in simple drawings or art forms.

3. Based on the St. Paul's advice regarding the Christian walk, share some of your observations on what it means to:

    A) Live in love
    B) Live as children of light
    C) Live in wisdom

• **RELATED SCRIPTURE SOURCES**

Ephesians 5:1-21

Love:	John 15:9-15	Romans 5:5	1 Corinthians 13
Light:	Matthew 5:16	John 1:4, 17:26	1 Thessalonians 5:5
Wisdom:	Psalm 51:6	Proverbs 9:9-12	James 1:2-5

• **NEW PERSPECTIVES**

Consider personal changes you can make and/or new steps you can take to be of service to others.

• **QUESTIONS TO BE RESOLVED**

(Can be listed on a separate page)

• **A PRAYER THOUGHT**

"We give thanks to You, Redeemer God, for our Lord Jesus Christ, who came in quietness and humility, but who will come again with power and for all to see. Our Lord Jesus' coming again is a two-edged sword. It comforts us, convinces us anew that Your grace is beyond measure. Yet is also confronts us, compels us to recognize our own unrighteousness. Let us put aside our false pride, confess our sins, and receive Your affirming love."

How Easy It is to Drift

Only a few weeks ago our entire family of children, grandchildren, a family friend, and my wife and I enjoyed another one of our annual vacations together. This year it revolved around a rented condominium on the seaside of North Myrtle Beach, South Carolina.

One morning following a late breakfast, we suddenly heard the strange but piercing sounds similar to sheep horns blasting from the lifeguard positions on the beach. It caused all of our family to rush to the balcony overlooking the beach, where we noticed the lifeguards frantically motioning to a lone swimmer with just his head bobbing in the waves about 300 yards offshore.

Their efforts were in vain, as the swimmer continued to refuse to follow their directions to come in to shore. Within moments two able lifeguards launched into the heavy surge and swam vigorously for about 15 or 20 minutes to reach the wayward swimmer. With the aid of an added speedboat, the vigilant guards forced the swimmer to the shore where an awaiting policeman read the swimmer's rights, handcuffed the reluctant man, and escorted him off the beach. Some of our youthful family members recognized having met the man earlier on the parking lot, where he appeared to be under the influence of alcohol or drugs. In his condition, he was unwilling to acknowledge the swift undertow and currents which were carrying him dangerously out to sea; he was unaware or unwilling to recognize his state of "lostness" and the imminent possibility of losing his life. We are reminded in such an incident how easy it is to drift and become unaware or insensitive to our "lostness." We think we can handle our life and ignore the safeguards. We are confident that we are sufficient in ourselves. Who has the right to caution us, or judge us, or to seek to redirect us back to rightful ways again? Sometimes even the most gracious invitation doesn't bring us to our senses.

One of my favorite parables of Jesus is found in Luke 14, the parable of the great banquet. A very wealthy man had prepared a lavish banquet and invited many guests. The day of the event, a servant is sent to tell people the feast was ready. But everyone begins to make excuses: weddings, business purchases, land deals – lots of things to do and all seemingly legitimate reasons to not attend the banquet.

The host is furious and gives a preposterous decision to the servant. He tells him to go into the streets and alleys of the town, and to bring in the poor, the crippled, the blind, and the lame. These were the marginalized people; the people with whom no one at the time wanted to be associated. Can you imagine how bizarre the banquet must have seemed? Along with the physically handicapped were criminals, the homeless, and drug addicts; a large table full of mangy, filthy, and seemingly uncouth social "rejects," none of whom were supposed to be there. And then we are told that it is a parable of the church! A bunch of losers and rejects?

Michael Yaconelli, in his intriguing book *Dangerous Wonder*, tells of a personal experience when he and his wife were remodeling their home. They decided to redo the tile in their kitchen. For a number of years they had volunteered with a Young Life Club in their town. A young man in the Club was having a hard year in school work and detention. They worked and guided this young man while his dad went through detox. His dad was an alcoholic, and he emotionally and physically abused the entire family.

The tile company was facing a shortage of personnel, and they couldn't lay the tile for many weeks. The company could only suggest the name of the young friend's father. Yaconelli yelled into the phone, "Absolutely not! That man is an alcoholic, knocks his family around, and I don't trust him!"

Two days later, however, he reluctantly agreed to hire the man suggested, but he told his wife, "I am going to watch him like a hawk. He's not going to cheat me." The estimate was for $350.

When the job was finished at 5 p.m., the tile layer walked into Yaconelli's office and handed in the bill saying, "A couple of years ago I was drinking too much and was at a very low point in my life. I mistreated my wife and family and especially my oldest son. But you and your wife spent a lot of time with him at a critical moment in his life. Shortly after that time, I went to AA and I've been sober ever since. Because of you and your wife, I still have a relationship with my son. I've never been able to thank you, but I am thanking you now." He handed in his bill for $350 marked "Paid in full" across the page.

Humiliated, Yaconelli slumped down in his chair, speechless. He concluded, "I was one who had been too busy to show up at the banquet, and he was one of the people who came."

The grace of God sure levels us all. All of us are broken; all of us are flawed; all of us are undeserving. There is no room for pride, a judgmental attitude, or arrogance. Each of us has had our debt "paid in full," and Jesus paid it all. Thanks be to God!

How Easy It is to Drift
Reflection/Quest Time

• **Exploring Questions for Discussion**
1. Have you ever drifted and become lost in your focus? Have you ever been insensitive to your "lostness?" Take another look. How did you overcome this situation? In what ways was your spiritual health altered?
2. Did your drift create a motivation to become a caregiver to individuals who have lost their way? If not, could it?

• **Related Scripture Sources**
    Luke Chapter 14   Hebrews 4:12-13
    Romans 8:25-34   Hebrews 4:15-16
    1 Corinthians 2:1-5

• **New Perspectives**
Consider personal changes you can make and/or new steps you can take to be of service to others.

• **Questions to be Resolved**
(Can be listed on a separate page)

• **A Prayer Thought**

"May the variety of traditions and customs of Your whole church become a multitude of lights to reveal the good news needed by people everywhere. May the variety of our ministries and service convey Your redemptive love and bind us ever closer to one another.

Grant us grace to unite in essentials, to accept diversity in non-essentials, and to love one another in all things."

CHAPTER V

THE CERTAINTY OF
God's Triumph

The last book of the Bible expresses the meaning of the Greeks symbols pictured above. God reveals, "I am the Alpha and the Omega, the first and the last, the beginning and the ending." (Revelation 22:13) The psalmist made it more personal, declaring, "For You, O Lord, have made me glad by Your work; at the works of Your hands I sing for joy." (Psalm 92:4) St. Paul proclaimed his confidence and thanksgiving: "Thanks be to God, who in Christ always leads us in triumphal procession, and through us spreads in every place the fragrance that comes from knowing Him." (2 Corinthians 2:14) Ultimately God's triumph is expressed in the certainty of the Lord's Second Coming. Your Lord is coming! Be ready!

FAITH IS THE ONLY
PREPARATION THAT YOU NEED

New Year's Eve and the entrance into a new millennium provides us with a sparkling vista of insight and opportunity. A few years ago, we had the joy of visiting one of our children and his family in Pasadena, California, during the New Year's holiday. While there, my son's neighbor invited us to attend the Rose Bowl Parade, which is an extravaganza of flowers, floats, music and well-known celebrities. It meant leaving early – while it was still dark – to travel to a spot on the parade route where we could see it all up close.

Nearby, along the parade route, was a group of college-age boys who had obviously arrived a day ahead of time to obtain a choice location. They were sitting on a conglomeration of imported stuffed chairs, sofas, and sleeping bags, and they had a cooler, a charcoal grill, and oodles of food and beverages. I envied their choice setting and mobile comforts. They were a rather enthusiastic bunch, and I began to realize that they had been consuming some strong beverages.

Ironically, by the time the parade started to pass, a strange silence had overtaken the boys. They were all asleep in their soft surroundings. They all missed the parade for which they had extensively prepared. What a parable of missed opportunity! Robert Louis Stevenson was correct when he said, "To miss the joy is to miss all."

I have often heard statements prefaced by the question, "Are you ready for this?" The question is a good one. How ready are we for what happens in our lives? We are often unprepared for the bad . . . and sometimes even for the good. Occasionally, I hear the comment, "I was caught off guard – I never expected something good to happen!"

A lack of preparedness can minimize the truly awesome experiences of life. We can become so negative that we expect the worst and are almost disappointed if it doesn't happen. The Lord wants a prepared and expectant people, ready to be "surprised by joy," as C.S. Lewis expressed it. Christ has called us to be adventurers who have trusted the future to Him and anticipate His interventions in the most unexpected places and situations.

The parable of the wise and foolish bridesmaids is the parable of preparedness for joy. (Matthew 25:1-13) It reveals the quality of unreserved, willing, hopeful anticipation Jesus desired in His disciples, and wants now in us. God is the One who breaks into life. He came to humankind in the Messiah. He will return again in the Second Coming – but He comes daily to each of us.

Jesus taught the parable of the bridesmaids at the end of his ministry in response to the disciples' frightened questions about the future. Would the Lord return? How soon? What would be the signs? What was going to happen to them?

The wisdom of the wise bridesmaids and the folly of the foolish bridesmaids was that some were prepared for the joy of the coming of the bridegroom and the others were not. Five had not brought extra oil for their lamps. Frustrated frenzy ensued. They tried to borrow oil from the five who were prepared but were refused. It was too late.

The thrust of the parable of the bridesmaids is: Are we prepared to live today as if it were our last? If the end purpose of our life is accomplished, we will not need to fear the end of life – neither the end of the world nor the end of our existence. Being filled with God's Spirit makes us ready-for-anything-believers. We can say, "Let life happen! Let it come with winter winds and its disappointments; its springtime and unanticipated delight; its arduous days and restless nights. We are ready! We are open to grow, agile to recoup, free to fall, willing to cut our losses and able to surge ahead."

Why is it that some miss what God wants to give? Many are unaware. For them, life moves aimlessly towards an uncertain end. But then a crisis may slap them awake! Thank God for life's crises which make us face reality. The tragedy, however, is that we can't get ready for a crisis in the midst of the crisis – we cannot borrow preparedness.

Here is God's personal word. Are we ready? Why not settle that once and for all? The tragic unpreparedness of the bridesmaids need not be our condition. We can be filled with the Spirit. (Ephesians 5:18) The result will be a new preparedness for life – now and forever. Right at this moment, the good news is being sounded, "Behold the Bridegroom is coming!" It's an exciting delight to be able to say, "Lord, I'm ready! Ready for anything and anyone! Lead on!"

Faith is the Only Preparation That You Need

Reflection/Quest Time

• **Exploring Questions for Discussion**

1. What does the parable of the bridesmaids say to you?
2. Can you recall a life crisis for which you were unprepared? What changes have you made in your life as a result?

• **Related Scripture Sources**

Matthew 25:1-13   Ephesians 5:18

• **New Perspectives**

Consider personal changes you can make and/or new steps you can take to be of service to others.

• **Questions to be Resolved**

(Can be listed on a separate page)

• **A Prayer Thought**

"What no eye has seen, nor ear heard, nor the human heart conceived, what God has prepared for those who love Him. " (1 Corinthians 2:9)

THE POWER OF HOSPITALITY
AND BIBLICAL GOODNESS

I am a student of ethics, of good and evil. This is the most ancient of inquiries, having roots in the Garden of Eden with the encounters of Adam and Eve. Cruelty has been called the "Nightmare of History." It haunts our consciousness in powerful exhibits of inhumanity such as the expose of the hideous humiliation and sexual abuse carried out by American troops in Abu Ghraib Prison in Iraq. Other recent examples include the behavior of some national leaders of countries in Africa who are dooming hundreds of thousands of their countrymen to death by starvation in the denial of donated food and assistance. Also, the CEO's of corporate America who have knowingly and ruthlessly distorted the financial truth of their companies in a greedy quest for personal gain which has resulted in the unemployment of thousands of employees and the evaporation of their life's savings and pensions. Cruelty comes in so many varieties. Even our candidates for the presidency speak of each other in evil terms with spins that cause good people to gasp for the truth in the midst of accusations.

In his book *Lest Innocent Blood Be Shed*, Philip Hallie includes an article entitled "From Cruelty To Goodness." He cites the residents of the French village of Le Chambon, who at grave risk to their lives, saved 6,000 Jews from the Nazis. For Hallie the contrary of being cruel is epitomized in the unambiguous and unpretentious goodness of the citizens of Le Chambon, who followed the positive biblical injunctions "Defend the Fatherless" and "Be Your Brother's Keeper" as well as the negative injunction "Thou shalt not murder or betray." For a millennia in history and literature, people have been torturing each other not only with hard weapons and actions but also with hard words.

The French Protestant village of Le Chambon saved the lives of about 6,000 people, most of them Jewish children whose parents had been murdered in the killing camps of Central Europe. Under the day-to-day threat of destruction by the German Armed SS, the town's people began saving children in the winter of 1940, after the fall of France, and they continued to do so until the war was over. They sheltered the refugees in their homes and in various houses they established especially for them; and they took many of them across the terrible mountains to neutral Geneva, Switzerland, which was in the teeth of the French and German police and military power.

The people of Le Chambon were poor, and the Huguenot faith to which they belonged is now a diminishing faith in Catholic and atheistic France. Nonetheless, their spiritual power and their capacity to act in union against the victimizers who surrounded them, was immense, and more than a match for the military power of those victimizers. They were the embodiment of Biblical goodness – the opposite of cruelty. They provide us with a picture of the power of hospitality, a central theme of the Bible, which was practiced by few others during the Holocaust. Goodness happened in Le Chambon.

Hallie recently received a letter from a woman who had been saved by the people of Le Chambon when she was a young girl. She wrote, "Never was there a question that the Chambonais would not share all they had with us, meager as it was. One Chambonais once told me that even if there was less, they still would want more for us." And she goes on: "If today we are not bitter people like most survivors it can only be due to the fact that we met people like the people of Le Chambon, who showed to us simply that life can be different, that there are people who care, that people can live together and even risk their own lives for their fellow man."

These people of Christian faith taught the refugees that goodness can conquer cruelty, that loving hospitality is an expression from the heart of God, as personified in Jesus, the good shepherd who gives His life for His sheep. One woman whose children were saved by the love and hospitality of this tiny French town concluded in a public forum in recent days, "The Holocaust was storm, lightning, thunder, wind, rain, yes. And Le Chambon was the rainbow." We are all challenged to be the rainbow of goodness in our time and place. Let God in. Let us begin. It is a matter of the heart.

THE POWER OF HOSPITALITY
AND BIBLICAL GOODNESS
REFLECTION/QUEST TIME

• EXPLORING QUESTIONS FOR DISCUSSION

1. The power of hospitality is a central message of the Bible, and as such is an expression from the heart of God. When have you been the recipient of the gift of hospitality?

2. Is there someone in your life who needs your loving hospitality?

3. If goodness can conquer cruelty, where in your neighborhood, community, or nation is goodness most needed? Are you personally willing to act to make a difference?

• RELATED SCRIPTURE SOURCES

Hospitality:	1 Timothy 3:1-7	1 Peter 4:8-11
Fatherless:	Isaiah 1:23	Psalm 10: 12-18
	Genesis 4:9-11	
Goodness:	Psalm 52:1	Romans 2:1-11
	Romans 11:22	Galations 5:22-26

• NEW PERSPECTIVES

Consider personal changes you can make and/or new steps you can take to be of service to others.

• QUESTIONS TO BE RESOLVED

(Can be listed on a separate page)

• A PRAYER THOUGHT

"We hear Your call to discipleship. Master, teach us the way we should go.

Present your bodies as a living sacrifice, hold and acceptable to God, which is your spiritual worship. Do not be conformed to this world, but be transformed by the renewal of your minds, that you may prove what is the will of God, what is good and acceptable and perfect.

Jesus said: This is My commandment, that you love one another as I have loved you. I chose you and appointed you that you should go and bear much fruit, and that your fruit should abide."

An Unexpected Truth: Christ's Promised Return Here on Earth

There are great moments in each of our lives when a special truth or enlightenment comes home to us by some unexpected surprise. A mother recently recounted her experience of her young son leaving his bedroom, and joining his parents in their bed and snuggling very close to them. He shared his fear of his bedroom. In taking her son back to his bed, she explained with confidence that he shouldn't be afraid because "God is in your bedroom." The response came back, "That may be, but I want to feel skin!" What a human moment when a person or two are together giving each other uninterrupted attention. We discover or rediscover an unexpected truth. These surprises can reap great benefits by avoiding doing business as usual.

Here we are at another significant moment in our technological history when the computer world is facing up to the realities of change as we gear up for the next generation. The computer comes to us as one of the most recent developmental watersheds of history. A recent speaker noted five of these watersheds, beginning with the ancient Greeks' contributions to literacy. Conveying ideas and information were transmitted by paper and ink. In the 15th century, the Guttenburg Press provided a new method of printing that replaced intensive labor to communicate knowledge and open us to the world of books. In the early 18th century, Samuel Morse invented the telegraph which conveyed news and messages from the speed of horses to the speed of light. Our concept of the neighborhood began to increase to include all those to whom we speak. In the last half of the 19th century, the photograph emerged and soon after the motion picture industry revolutionized communications and education. The TV has surfaced as the most dominant social influence in our society for better and worse. In the 20th century, the computer conveying text, sound, images, a filing system, and a means of communication has transformed the mental landscape of the world so much that it foretells the end of the university as we know it in the advent of distance learning.

As inheritors of these significant watersheds of history, we have welcomed eagerly technological innovations that make our daily tasks easier. But often times this is done at the expense of our real human needs – including the need "to feel skin." Zechariah 1:7, 12-18 addresses living with ease, where we read that the

Lord addressed Zechariah saying, "I am extremely angry with the nations that are at ease; for while I was only a little angry, they made the disaster worse." The Gospel lesson in Matthew 25:14-30 encourages us to look at our talents — referring to natural aptitudes and abilities - and use them whenever given the opportunity. The Epistle lesson emerges from 1 Thessalonians 5:1-11, alerting us to what it means to live in expectation and hope by anticipating a surprise, namely, the return of Jesus Christ.

How easily we have become numb to the gifts of technology, thoughtlessly going about business as usual. Is the same true of our relationship with God? The Bible has revealed that the Word became flesh in the person of Jesus, and He transforms the lives of those who have invited Him into their lives. Living in the light of Jesus' promised return here on earth is a surprise encompassing personal and global fulfillment. On that surprise day of God's choosing, He will come! Jesus urges us to not live lives of complacency. Rather, we are to "keep awake," to be prepared for the inevitable crises of life, and for the crisis which will accompany His return. We are to live as those who expect the advent of God into our lives.

An Unexpected Truth:
Christ's Promised Return
Here On Earth
Reflection/Quest Time

• **Exploring Questions for Discussion**
1. What can you do to heed Jesus' advice to "keep awake" in the light of His promised return?
2. Have we become too comfortable and/or behaved too confidently in our day-to-day lives? Have technological improvements contributed to this behavior?

• **Related Scripture Sources**

Zechariah 1:7, 12-18   Matthew 25:14-30
1 Thessalonians 5:1-11   Revelation 22:7-14

• **New Perspectives**
Consider personal changes you can make and/or new steps you can take to be of service to others.

• **Questions to be Resolved**
(Can be listed on a separate page)

• A Prayer Thought

"God of hope, You comfort us through our Savior's promise to return in glory at the end of time. As we await the coming of the Prince of Peace, let us not despair. We long for You to inspire all the nations and peoples of the world to turn to cooperation and nurture, rather than to hatred and destruction. God of faith, love and hope, to You and to You alone we pray: For You are our God, the only God, forever and ever."

The Journey
We Will Call Home

Annually, we observe Mother's Day and Christian Home Week soon. How can much be said these days without some reference to the awesome tragedy and the deep implications suggested by the deadly explosion in the Federal Building in Tulsa Oklahoma? Families and homes have been blasted apart. In a negative sense, the revelation is truly awesome. The whole experience is and will continue to be both real and symbolic of the evil, which truly lurks in the hearts of some and in other ways in the hearts of each of us. There are voices of hope, which suggest that this holocaust in the heartland of America will help trigger a spiritual revival in the hearts of our country. Other signs today of spiritual renewal support the idea. Earlier awakenings in the spiritual life of our nation suggest that in a different time and with different faces an awesome transformation of spirit, lifestyle, morals, and values can take place if we stimulate our souls and venture with expectations.

In visiting one of our favorite seaside locations on the New Jersey shore recently we were attracted by a very prominent sign, which announced daily trips for "Whale Watching, Dophin Watching and Bird Watching." I have heard so much about the excitement engendered by those who have gone on boat excursions off the coast of Maine and Massachusetts.

Before too much time and conversation elapsed, my wife and I and some family friends found ourselves purchasing tickets and getting on the boat expecting especially to watch whales. We did this despite the fact that we were told by some sea lovers that this time of the year may be to early to enjoy the spectacle of those special whale performers. The day was beautiful and clear, the tour boat was gracious as we cruised toward the expected sightings, and the captain and crew frequently encouraged us over the loudspeaker to be alert and help them to search the horizon with our binoculars as we approached the known habitat of the whales. Despite our hopes and expectations we never got to see a whale. Moreover, no dophins provided their customary friendly visits to the side of the boat. At least the bird watching came through as predicted with the ever-present seagulls. An occasional loon and a few other varieties of our feathered friends joined them. It was a great trip even though we never satisfied our hearts desire to "watch the whales,' Maybe next time.

But we did have an experience, which stirred us to our depths. The magnitude of the sea, the majesty of the skies, the creative genius of God, and the distinctive role of man in the total creation welled up within us. While we visited the home of the whale, our challenge as human beings is to be at home with God. Some powerful words describe the key qualities and experiences which help us find our way home such as awe, love, woe, care, joy, save and life and home.

THE JOURNEY WE WILL CALL HOME
REFLECTION/QUEST TIME

• EXPLORING QUESTIONS FOR DISCUSSION
1. What does it mean to be at home with God?
2. There are some powerful words, which describe the key qualities, and experiences, which help us find our way home as found in the hymn on the next page. They are awe, grace, love, woe, care, joy, save, life, and home. Take each word and write a sentence or two applying them to the environment of our heavenly home and the journey home.

• RELATED SCRIPTURE SOURCES
John 14:23   Ephesians 3:12-21
Ecclesiastes 12:5-6

• NEW PERSPECTIVES
Consider personal changes you can make and/or new steps you can take to be of service to others.

• QUESTIONS TO BE RESOLVED
(Can be listed on a separate page)

• A PRAYER THOUGHT
TEN THOUSAND TIMES TEN THOUSAND
"Bring near your great salvation,
O Lamb of sinners slain;
Fill up the roll of your elect,
Then take your pow'r and reign!
Appear, Desire of nations,
Your exiles long for home;
Show in the heav'n your promised sign;
Then, Prince and Savior, come."

One of the hymns in the Moravian Book of Worship question very vividly the relationship of the creature with the Creator and the journey we call home. Perhaps we can catch the message:

"God of the sparrow
God of the whale
God of the swirling stars
    How does the creature say awe?
    How does the creature say praise?

God of the rainbow
God of the whale
God of the empty grave
    How does the creature say grace?
    How does the creature say thanks?

God of the neighbor
God of the foe
God of the pruning hook
    How does the creature say love?
    How does the creature say peace?

God of the earthquake
God of the storm
God of the trumpet blast
    How does the creature cry woe?
    How does the creature cry save?

God of the hungry
God of the sick
God of the prodigal_
    How does the creature say care?
    How does the creature say life?

God of the ages
God near at hand
God of the loving heart
    How do your children say joy?
    How do your children say home?

It is time to come home to God."

CHAPTER VI
Seasonal Emphases

ADVENT

CHRISTMAS

EPIPHANY

LENT

EASTER

PENTECOST

This final chapter addresses the themes of the church year. They highlight in their daily scriptural foundations the unfolding purpose of God expressed in the family of faith involving community and commitment. The chalice portrayed above captures the qualities elevated in Psalm 75:8 – "For in the hand of the Lord there is a cup." Jesus refers to this cup in 1 Corinthians 11:25-26, "This cup is the new covenant in My blood. Do this, as often as you drink it, in remembrance of Me. For as often as you eat this bread and drink the cup, you proclaim the Lord's death until He comes."

As Henri Nouwen explains in his book *Can You Drink the Cup*, "Drinking the cup is an act of selfless love, an act of immense trust, short of surrender to a God who will give what we need when we need it." Are you prepared to drink this cup?

LET GOD SHOW YOU
HIS STUFF THIS ADVENT

What is your favorite time of year? For me, it's Thanksgiving and Christmas. I can almost smell and see the roasted turkey.

The actress Helen Hayes once told a story about cooking her first Thanksgiving turkey. She explained that she wasn't a very good cook, but after several years of marriage, she decided to try preparing a turkey on her own.

She sat her husband and son down before the meal and said, "This may not come out exactly the way you want it to. If it's not a good turkey, don't say a thing. Without any comment, just stand up from the table, and we'll go to the nearest restaurant to eat."

A few moments later, Helen walked into the dining room with the turkey. Her husband and son were already standing with their coats and hats on!

Our expectations definitely control our conduct.

We conduct out life and daily affairs based on what we expect from them. Kids provide a classic example. If you have grade-school children in your house, you have no problem getting them up on Christmas morning. As parents, most of us go to bed on Christmas Eve and pray, "Oh, God, let them sleep!"

But the day after New Year's, when those same kids have to go back to school, it's an entirely different matter. Why? Conduct is controlled and influenced by our expectations.

In our community of Nazareth, our borough employees have already placed picturesque pine trees on poles surrounding our town square in getting ready for the approaching Christmas season. Pretty soon they will be erecting the rustic stable and inserting the customary figures of the Nativity. Many people and families visit the site during the Christmas season to view the baby, born in a stable, who changed the world forever.

Above the humble crèche is the illuminated star. It projects for all of us the question, "What if you follow a star and find a stable?" In Matthew, Chapter 2, we read the story of the Wise Men following the star. What happens when all of a sudden, after thinking that something grand and glorious would be at the other end, you end up in the back yard of a barn? And there, instead of a place with a king on a throne, you find a baby held by his mother? It's nothing like what you had anticipated.

How is your conduct affected by the outcome of your expectations?

I look ahead this year to Christmas Day, but I realize it is with different expectations. For over thirty-five years, I have received a phone from a previous parishioner in Ohio early each Christmas morning. He extends his well wishes in the fashion of a hearty, "Merry Christmas!"

This tradition began in the harvest season of the year when in the field around this man's home, the corn was being harvested by a farmer and put into the farm wagon. Unknown to the farmer, the young but oldest son of this Ohio family was attracted to the moving tractor and wagon, and inadvertently tripped and fell under the wheels.

The young man was rushed to the hospital. I was called to his bedside as doctors fervently sought to determine what could be done to save his life. Question marks and fear were embedded on the faces of the parents and medical staff. Only time would tell the outcome. I went home later to assume some responsibilities.

After going to bed that night, I awakened about 2 a.m., redressed, and returned to the hospital, aware of the intensity and shattered expectations these faithful parents must have been experiencing. I found them in their anxious vigil. Fortunately, the boy survived the crushing experience and grew into a robust adult.

These Christmas morning greetings for over more than three decades expressed echoes of appreciation from the child's parent who never forgot the bonding experience they experienced in the midst of uncertainty.

This year, Christmas Day will be different for me, because parishioner Jim won't be making the call. A few months ago I received the news of his death.

Pastor John Maxwell of San Diego suggests there is an answer to the question of, "What do you do when you follow a star and find a stable?" The Wise Men are our model: "When wise men find a stable, they offer their very best to God. When wise men find a stable, they change their direction."

Yes, it happens to everybody once in a while in our own corner of the world, far beyond the distant hills of Palestine. As we examine our attitudes and actions in this season of Thanksgiving, we find inspiration, for there are some very nice and wonderful ways to deal with the unexpected in our lives.

This is a message for those of us whose dreams have not been fulfilled, at least not in the way we'd hoped. Look for God. Offer God your best. Change your direction. We are influenced by our expectations.

LET GOD SHOW YOU
HIS STUFF THIS ADVENT
REFLECTION/QUEST TIME

• **EXPLORING QUESTIONS FOR DISCUSSION**
1. What does it mean for today, and this important season in the church year, to "Prepare the way of the Lord?"
2. Can Advent become a time to change old patterns, such as the materialism and accumulation imbedded in our culture and our own personal lives?

• **RELATED SCRIPTURE SOURCES**
Matthew 3:1-10

• **NEW PERSPECTIVES**
Consider personal changes you can make and/or new steps you can take to be of service to others.

• **QUESTIONS TO BE RESOLVED**
(Can be listed on a separate page)

• **A PRAYER THOUGHT**

"Christ, the Light of the world, empower us to shine as lights in this dark world of sin.

Christ, the Creative Word, by whom all things were made, lead us into good stewardship of creation that our children and we may preserve and enjoy the world entrusted to us.

Christ, the Living Truth, give us the spirit of wisdom and understanding that sees beyond temporal values to discern your truth and to declare it.

Christ, our Righteous Judge, give us courage to stand by the poor, the meek, and the oppressed; and strengthen our support for all who are their advocates."

WHEN THE JESUS OF HISTORY BECOMES THE CHRIST OF EXPERIENCE

Christmas! What is it all about? Beyond the spectacle and the spending, can we get to the heart of these dramatic festive moments, delightful for so many and dreaded by others? Christmas is observed in widely different patterns, ranging from spiritual foundations to superficial frivolities. What is Christmas to you?

For me the image of the red kettle and the tinkling bell has embedded itself into my personal experience. These are the symbols of the ministry of the Salvation Army to the lost and the unfortunate of our community, nation and the world. For over a decade, I have been part of the army of volunteers who have rung the bell welcoming the donations of Christmas shoppers. Each year I am lured to stand in the brisk air of December outside a busy store or in the indoor movement of people within a mall.

What an experience to observe the parade of responses and reactions exhibited by the adults and children at the sight of the kettle and the ringing of the bell. Some approach the giving of their donations with a smile and gentle greeting of "Merry Christmas." In contrast, there are those who look the other way or who are preoccupied in a glance at some simple distraction – anything to avoid a visit to the red kettle. Select groups of parents make it a family affair with all of the family sharing and caring as they individually deposit their money.

Perhaps the most touching in these choice experiences is for some individuals to come up to the kettle, almost as if to worship with their gift, and to testify with appreciation to how the Salvation Army helped out their family when they needed it the most. Others speak of the presence of the Salvation Army in faraway places during their wartime military service. They don't forget. The Christmas caravan of givers and passers-by made up of the friendly, the appreciative, the generous, the needy, the indifferent, and even the antagonistic, gives witness to the expression that "Sharing is caring."

More than any experience of the season, I welcome, in fact cherish, the opportunity to be a host at the Salvation Army kettles of care. These are moments when I am brought closer to the experience of what Christmas is all about. It is a renewing experience to draw more realistically to the Christ of Christmas.

The fact of Christmas is that the Jesus of history was born in Bethlehem of Judea. However, the dynamic of Christmas is fulfilled in believers when the Jesus of history becomes the Christ of experience within one's personal faith discovery.

147

In the words of Scripture, "Unto us is born a Savior who is Christ the Lord."

One of the hymns used in Moravian Advent services keynotes the theme:

> Once He came in blessing
> All our sins redressing . . .
> Still He comes within us.
> Still His voice would win us.
> From the sins that hurt us.

Truly experiencing Christmas is to experience Christ – to recognize that the birth of Jesus is part of God's sharing and caring for you and me. The humble circumstances of the birth are like the humbling of our wills in receiving Christ as Savior in our lives. One passage in the Bible encourages us to "Humble yourselves therefore under the mighty hand of God, that He may exalt you in due time. Cast all your anxieties upon Him, because He cares for you." (1 Peter 5:6) Do you want to make Christmas real in your life? This year offers you a fresh start. The last two verses of the Advent hymn come to guide us:

> Thus if we have known Him,
> Not ashamed to own Him,
> Nor have spurned Him coldly,
> But will trust Him boldly,
> He will then receive us,
> Heal us, and forgive us.
> Those who then are loyal
> Find a welcome royal.
> Come then, O Lord Jesus,
> From our sins release us;
> Let us here confess you
> Till in Heaven we bless you.

WHEN THE JESUS OF HISTORY
BECOMES THE CHRIST OF EXPERIENCE
REFLECTION/QUEST TIME

• EXPLORING QUESTIONS FOR DISCUSSION
1. How would you describe the meaning of Christmas?
2. Can you identify a moment that affected your life in a transformative way?
3. What qualities constitute "humbling yourselves under the mighty hand of God"?

• RELATED SCRIPTURE SOURCES
1 Peter 5:6   Luke 2:8-20
Isaiah 9:6

• NEW PERSPECTIVES
Consider personal changes you can make and/or new steps you can take to be of service to others.

• QUESTIONS TO BE RESOLVED
(Can be listed on a separate page)

• A PRAYER THOUGHT
"By Your tender mercy you cause the bright dawn of salvation to rise on us, to give light to those who sit in darkness and in the shadow of death, to guide our feet into the way of peace."

BE PREPARED TO RECEIVE GOD'S GIFT OF EXPECTANCY

Shortly before Thanksgiving Day, I wandered randomly through a nearby department store looking to buy a belt. The customers were few at the time, and I could hear the first of the Christmas carols coming over the loudspeaker. It seemed like the quiet before the storm. The more I walked the more I became aware, actually overwhelmed, at the huge piles of "stuff" poised to attract the predictable Christmas shoppers.

"Stuff" is the best way I can describe the unending accumulation of things I saw and what I felt deep inside as I asked myself, "What is the meaning of all this?" Quietly I recalled the catchy comment of someone who said while noting our vain efforts to accumulate things: "He that has the most when he dies, wins." How vain can we become? There are times when the word "stuff" has been used to mean something of knowledge or value when saying, "He knows his stuff" or in speaking of a noble team effort, "they are showing their stuff".

But, during this special time called Advent, even though we seem swamped in a wilderness of things and a frenzy of activities, we would do well to stop long enough to ask the meaning of all of this "stuff."

During the Thanksgiving weekend, members of our family and some friends spent time in beautiful and historic Lexington, Virginia. Washington and Lee University, the home of Stonewall Jackson, and numerous other historic building sites provide a major attraction for tourists from around the world. Add to this the appealing campus of Virginia Military Institute and the George C. Marshall Museum and Research Library, and one recognizes that this is a special place. We became refreshed again reviewing the great attributes and accomplishments of Marshall, one of the greatest generals in our history. This Nobel Prize winner, identified as "a Soldier of Peace," had to fight for his nation's interests and some-times its very life – both as Chief of Staff during World War II and as Secretary of State in the raw, cold, hungry, postwar world that followed.

In the shadows of victory, Marshall recognized above all others that starva-tion and suffering in the war torn cities of Britain, France, the Low Countries, Germany, and Eastern Europe were wrecking people with despair and hopeless-ness. A disaster too dreadful to contemplate threatened this devastated corner of civilization. Out of these realities, the Marshall Plan was born. Against all odds at home and abroad, George Marshall motivated and led America, in the midst of our victory and abundance to a new conscience of brotherhood and humanity. In a world of over-paid heroes and untrustworthy officials, Marshall maintained his principles, though not without pain, struggle, and suffering. As a result a new world emerged.

Scriptural verses often used during the Advent season refer to the coming of Christ saying, "In those days John the Baptist appeared in the wilderness of Judea, proclaiming, "Repent, for the kingdom of heaven has come near." He states, "I baptized you with water for repentance, but one who is more powerful than I . . . will baptize you with the Holy Spirit and fire . . . the chaff He will burn with unquenchable fire." (Matt. 3: 1-12)

In the wilderness of our materialism, accumulation, and the gifting of "stuff," we would do well to hear the voice crying, "Prepare the way of the Lord" rather than following the impulses drawing us to prepare for Christmas by wandering around in malls. Isn't it a time to repent, and to allow the Lord to sift us as wheat?

God can baptize us with His Spirit even as the chaff ["stuff"] is burned away. The vital coming of Christ into our lives can stir us in new directions so as to truly know that "the kingdom of Heaven has come near."

BE PREPARED TO RECEIVE
GOD'S GIFT OF EXPECTANCY
REFLECTION/QUEST TIME

• EXPLORING QUESTIONS FOR DISCUSSION
1. Where have your expectations led you? What have you discovered about yourself along the way?
2. How might changing your expectations change your future life course?
3. How are your expectations helping to fulfill the purpose of God's gift expectancy in the season of Christ's Advent?

• RELATED SCRIPTURE SOURCES

    Matthew 3:1-10   Matthew 25:31-32

    John 1:14   I John 1:1

    John 4:2-3

• NEW PERSPECTIVES

Consider personal changes you can make and/or new steps you can take to be of service to others.

• QUESTIONS TO BE RESOLVED

(Can be listed on a separate page)

• A Prayer Thought

"Thou didst leave Thy throne and Thy kingly crown
When Thou camest to earth for me.
But in Bethlehem's home there was found no room
For Thy holy nativity.
O come to my heart, Lord Jesus:
There is room in my heart for Thee!

Heaven's arches rang when the angels sang,
Proclaiming Thy royal degree,
But in lowly birth didst Thou come to earth
And in great humility.
O come to my heart, Lord Jesus:
There is room in my heart for Thee!

When the heavens shall ring and the angels sing
At Thy coming to victory.
Let Thy voice call me home saying, "Yet there is room,
There is room at My side for thee."
And my heart shall rejoice, Lord Jesus,
Then Thou comest and callest me."

PREPARING FOR
THE BIG DAY

Over the last couple of months, our family has grown increasingly aware of the fact that one of our sons was looking forward to the anticipated day of the annual New York City Marathon. He was preparing in numerous ways: His daily runs of increasing length; his detailed attention to diet; and his cautious view in controlling body weight. By choice his business, family, and vacation schedules had to include being faithful to a regimen which would make possible the successful finishing of the required 26 miles of running on the day of the Marathon race.

Last Sunday, the long awaited day finally arrived and he joined almost 30,000 runners from around the world who were in astounding physical condition. Some exceptional runners ran to win. Most runners ran just to participate and hoped to finish. Our son finished the race, received his marathon medal, and came home exhausted and exhilarated. The achievement was enough for full satisfaction but the impact of the experience was hard for him to put into words. The massive enthusiasm of the hundreds of thousands of spectators, the medical aid and personal care given by oodles of volunteers, and the many seemingly disadvantaged runners with physical handicaps including blindness left our son speechless.

The Scriptures that are read during Advent refer to the Day of the Lord, a common conception found in the Old Testament. In the New Testament Gospel and Epistle lessons (Matthew 25:1-13 and I Thessalonians 4:13-18), the Day of the Lord is connected with the Second Coming of Christ. Pictorial dreams and visions of what would happen when God breaks into time are presented. For example, St. Paul states, ". . . the Lord Himself, with a cry of command, with the archangel's call and with the sound of God's trumpet, will descend from Heaven, and the dead in Christ will rise first. Then we who are alive, who are left, will be caught up in the clouds together with them to meet the Lord in the air; and so we will be with the Lord forever. Therefore encourage one another with these words."

We would do well to live more in the consciousness of the coming of the Lord than we are inclined to do. Every generation of the people of God is called to live in the hope of His coming, not in fear or forecasts, but with the undergirding sense that this is what history is about.

In the parable of Jesus found in Matthew 25:1-13, this same message is expressed in terms of a wedding involving five wise and five foolish bridesmaids. At midnight the joyous cry rings out, "The bridegroom is coming." Half the brides-maids are unprepared without oil in their lamps. The unprepared could not bor-row from the prepared. Three of the saddest sayings in the parables of Jesus are found here: (1) "Our lamps are out." (2) "The door was shut." and (3) "I do not know you." This is illustrative of God's judgment which is unequivocal and irre-versible. Clearly we cannot succeed on borrowed faith. The Christian community asks itself, "What does it mean to anticipate the Lord's coming?" And the Lord gives the answer – faithfulness. Jesus urges us, "Watch." That is, be prepared.

Preparing for the Big Day
Reflection/Quest Time

• **Exploring Questions for Discussion**

1. Can you think of events in your life for which you have planned for weeks, months, or a lifetime?

2. How prepared are you for the Lord's coming?

3. What steps can you take now to prepare?

• **Related Scripture Sources**

      1 Thessalonians 4:15-18   Mark 13:14-17

      Matthew 25:1-13   1 Corinthians 15:20-28

      Matthew 24:3-14; 32-44   Revelation 22:6-17

• **New Perspectives**

Consider personal changes you can make and/or new steps you can take to be of service to others.

• **Questions to be Resolved**

(Can be listed on a separate page)

• **A Prayer Thought**

"God of hope, You comfort us through our Savior's promise to return in glory at the end of time:

As we await the coming of the Prince of Peace, let us not despair. We long for You to inspire all the nations and peoples of the world to turn to cooperation and nurture, rather than to hatred and destruction.

God of faith, love and hope, to You and to You alone we pray:

For You are our God, the only God, forever and ever."

LOSING SIGHT
OF THE BIG PICTURE

My wife and I recently visited Hershey Park's Christmas lighting display and the entertainment attractions of rides, refreshments, and costumed animal characters walking among the crowds. The park was buzzing with people and dazzling lights, and the winter cold permeated the atmosphere.

At one point, my wife and I each got focused on two different displays. Without realizing it, we became separated and were lost to each other. Searching for each other eventually became a useless exercise, and gradually getting colder we each made our separate ways back to our distant car. Realizing what we had done created an awkward silence, as we drove away in our car.

Entering this magnetic season of Advent, we live between Christ's First and Second Advent. W. H. Auden noted that this is a temporary time period, only "for the time being," but certainly one of "the hardest times of all." In Christ, the redemption of the world is underway, yet that redemption remains in large part hidden, still awaiting the final consummation.

Christmas is about a baby. The second coming is something else. We stammer when we try to speak of it. As Cornelius Platinga, Jr. points out, the literature describing the Second Advent is apocalyptic - "It is an unveiling of the world that lies behind this world. It is a revelation that tells about the transition from this age to the next." He notes that the transition is rough; it is so full of emergency.

According to the Bible, everything will break loose with the return of Jesus Christ. In the midst of chaos, people will see "the Son of man coming in a cloud with power and great glory." (Matthew 24:30) He's the incoming Lord; He's the oncoming Lord. He has the power to judge and the power to save, and when He comes the second time He will be too big to miss.

At the end times, He will be "God without disguise," as C. S. Lewis once wrote. He will come at us so unmistakably that He "will strike either irresistible love or irresistible horror into every creature." This has been called the climax of the human drama.

So why does the Second Coming make some of us squirm? Perhaps we have trouble with the literature or we can't figure out God's schedule. Or is it possible that many of us have been so secularized that our view and experience of the world has jaded our outlook, and in our excitement of worldly interest and anxieties we have become lost in the lure of the immediate. We lose sight of the big picture.

Jesus, in speaking to the people of God, told the parable of the fig tree, which only produced leaves and no figs. (Luke 13:6-9) There was no fruitfulness, and the tree was discarded.

We are called during Advent to a sense of expectancy in order to be fruitful and alert. (Luke 21:34) Perhaps "for the time being," we would do well to reflect on acting as the Advent hymn suggests, "O come to my heart, Lord Jesus, there is room in my heart for Thee."

Losing Sight of the Big Picture
Reflection/Quest Time

• Exploring Questions for Discussion
1. Have you lost sight of the big picture?
2. What steps are you willing to take in your life to prepare for the Second Coming of Christ?
3. In what spiritual practices do you engage in order to be fruitful in the reality of the Kingdom?

• Related Scripture Sources

Luke 13:1-9	Matthew 24:29-31
Luke 21:34	Matthew 24:36

• New Perspectives
Consider personal changes you can make and/or new steps you can take to be of service to others.

• Questions to be Resolved
(Can be listed on a separate page)

• A Prayer Thought

"Gracious God, this Advent season stirs a longing to have Christ come alive within us, yet we allow ourselves to become enslaved to cynicism, selfishness, and greed. In a season for freely giving and receiving, we tend to live by debt and obligation. We rush from task to task, scarcely opening our eyes to the peace and beauty around us. We glory in the visions of the old man Zechariah in the temple, which were fulfilled in his wife, Elizabeth; but our ministry to the elderly in our midst falls short. We sing of One who was laid in a borrowed manger, but we ignore the poor and homeless among us. We decry the violence of a wicked king, yet we are too often silent in the face of abuse and injustice around us. For these and all our sins, forgive us, we pray, gracious God.

Comfort, comfort my people, says your God. Speak tenderly to them and proclaim that they have suffered long enough, that their penalty is paid, and their sins are forgiven.

The grace of God has appeared, bringing salvation to all. Christ Jesus gave Himself for us that He might redeem us from all iniquity and purify a people of His own. Thanks be to God!"

ARE WE ON A JOURNEY
TO THE LAST NOEL?

The Advent Christmas season captivates millions of people in all walks and circumstances of life, and in remote spots of the earth. "I'll Be Home for Christmas" is a seasonal tune that summarizes a great deal of sentiment, expressing the wish to be home with loved ones and familiar customs at Christmas.

I vividly remember one particular Christmas, as special as it could be under the circumstances. We lived in tents – hot by day and cold by night – supplied with the basics of food, clothing, and shelter.

On Christmas Day, we walked into Casablanca to an Army hospital complex where we enjoyed a festive meal with turkey and the trimmings, and worshiped in a large tent erected for that purpose. The efforts were appreciated, but nothing could take the place of being home for Christmas.

But a striking difference in that faraway place was noticed as we walked through the streets of Casablanca on the way to, and departing from, our Christmas observances. I immediately became aware of the numbers of people who seemed to wander aimlessly in city streets. Some pushed rickety carts with meager or nonexistent contents. Clusters of blind and lame people dressed in Arabic garb sat along walls and fences begging in desperation for food and money.

As night drew on, countless people chose their spots and crouched motionlessly to spend another night without shelter or a place they could call home. For the first time in my life, I saw people eagerly seeking to claim the garbage of the Army mess hall after our Christmas meal.

Christmas of 1945 became a personal landmark, giving me a new perspective. It dawned on me that the simple family of Joseph and pregnant Mary assumed a nomadic existence in search of a place to stay on their journey into Bethlehem of Judea.

No Holiday Inn was available. Their dress matched closely what native Semitic people in Casablanca wear today and have been wearing for centuries. Long flowing garb covers most of their bodies, shielding them from the blustery winds, and gusts of sweeping sand.

This humble couple sought earnestly the hospitality of the road and a residency that would assure some reasonable comfort during the impending birth of Jesus.

I was introduced to the fragile existence that these Middle Eastern travelers must endure. The emerging class of homeless people in this country and around the world experience similar complications and hardship.

Here we are in the middle of the Advent season heralding the "coming of Christ." In essence, we are in a spiritual nomadic journey between the first Noel and the last Noel – that is, the first coming of Christ in His birth and the final coming of Christ commonly known as the "Second Coming."

The Bible paints some vivid pictures of Jesus' return to earth "on the clouds." The Biblical authors make a terribly important point with this symbol; one day ". . . at the name of Jesus every knee should bend . . . and every tongue confess that Jesus Christ is Lord." (Philippians 2:10) That is why Christians hope for the Second Coming of Christ.

The Christian story, with its roots in the journey to Bethlehem of Judea, has its future in a final journey home at the end of time. In the words of Scripture, "But in accordance with His promise, we wait for new heavens and a new earth, where righteousness is at home." (2 Peter 3:13)

A stimulating Advent hymn describes it best:

"Thou didst leave Thy throne and Thy kingly crown when Thou camest to earth for me; Born in Bethlehem's home there was found no room for Thy holy nativity . . . O come to my heart Lord Jesus; there is room in my heart for Thee!

When the heavens shall ring, and the angels sing at Thy coming to victory, Let Thy voice call me home, saying "Yet there is room, there is room at My side for thee." And my heart shall rejoice, Lord Jesus, When Thou comest and callest for me."

ARE WE ON A JOURNEY
TO THE LAST NOEL?
REFLECTION/QUEST TIME

- **EXPLORING QUESTIONS FOR DISCUSSION**
1. How is our conduct controlled and influenced by the outcome of our expectations?
2. What if you follow a star and find a stable?
3. Can you list some ways in which you have dealt with the unexpected in your life?

- **RELATED SCRIPTURE SOURCES**
    Matthew – Chapter 2   Philippians 2:10

- **NEW PERSPECTIVES**
Consider personal changes you can make and/or new steps you can take to be of service to others.

- **QUESTIONS TO BE RESOLVED**
(Can be listed on a separate page)

- **A PRAYER THOUGHT**

"By the tender mercy of our God, the dawn from on high has broken upon us, to give light to those who sit in darkness and in the shadow of death.

To guide our feet into the way of peace.

For unto us a Child is born,

Unto us a Son is given.

God so loved the world that He gave His only Son, so that everyone who believes in Him may not perish but may have eternal life. Indeed, God did not send the Son into the world to condemn the world, but in order that the world might be saved through Him.

Thanks be to God for this gift beyond words!

My eyes have seen Your salvation,

Which You have prepared in the presence of all peoples."

STARTING OVER WITH GOD

One of the fascinating books currently being read in our home is the New York Times bestseller *River Horse* by William Least Heat-Moon.

In his most ambitious journey, the author sets off aboard a small boat from the Atlantic at New York Harbor in hopes of entering the Pacific Ocean off of Oregon. He and his companion struggle to cover some 5,000 miles, confronting massive floods, dangerous weather, and their own doubts whether they can complete the trip. Eventually, the hard days yield to incomparable pleasures – generous strangers, landscapes, riverscapes, and hilarious encounters with local eccentrics.

When traveling though Pennsylvania, the writer is captivated by the unusual varieties of strange names given to towns. He loves the flatness of imagination of town names which seem to come from some lost list of seven cardinal virtues of commerce: Frugality, Prosperity, Economy, Industry, Enterprise, Energy and Progress.

But the places he likes the most are the loony ones which make you ask "What in God's name were they thinking of?" Moosic, Blawnox, Nanty Glo, Orgisonia, Porkey, Equinunk, Coripon, Turnip Hole, Skunk, and (of course) old Zelienople, once the chicken dinner capital of western Pennsylvania.

Sometimes Bible names and passages can give a reader the same impression. In this Lenten season, we are pointed to the third chapter of the Gospel of St. John, where we encounter a man with a strange name identified with an elite religious group. He is obviously on a special quest – a journey of the soul. Nicodemus was a Pharisee, "a ruler of the Jews." What a strange name; in fact, it's almost a turnoff. But, then, we read about Nicodemus' life.

As Eugene Peterson writes in The Message:

Late one night [Nicodemus] visited Jesus and said, "Rabbi, we all know you're a teacher straight from God. No one could do all the God-pointing, God-revealing acts You do if God weren't in it."

Jesus said, "You're absolutely right. Take it from me what I'm pointing to – to God's kingdom."

"How can anyone," said Nicodemus, "be born who has already been born and grown up? You can't re-enter your mother's womb and be born again. What are You saying with this 'born from above' talk?"

Jesus said, "Don't be surprised when I tell you that you had to be born from above – out of this world, so to speak. You know well enough how the wind blows this way and that. You hear it rustling through the trees, but you have no idea where it comes from or where it is headed next. That's the way it is with everyone born from above by the wind of God, the Spirit of God."

Spiritual birth is something God accomplishes in us, not something we do. This is a miracle that only God can accomplish. The spiritual rebirth is mysterious and as impossible to see as the wind. Yet, like the wind, the work of the Spirit, though invisible, is real.

God is still working on me – and on you – even when we are not aware of it. The activity of God's spirit does not end with a moment of rebirth. God's spirit continues to guide, nurture, and protect us – in and for eternal life. We are born-again – and again and again.

Jesus uses a basic earthly category – human birth – to illuminate a profound spiritual reality, "Born again!" The phrase is arresting and fresh, alive with meaning. Another chance, starting over, new life! Is it possible? That is exactly what Jesus is saying.

The name Nicodemus may continue to sound strange to us, like the quaint names of settlements in Pennsylvania, but the experience or the fresh new encounter of the reality and beauty as seen with new eyes, a new heart, can result in a newborn person. Let us see Jesus again in this season of Lent, lifted up by the presence of the cross which calls each of us in love with new life.

Welcome to a journey not by boat in an adventure across the nation, but by a spiritual birth emerging from the heart and purpose of God for you and me.

STARTING OVER WITH GOD
REFLECTION/QUEST TIME

• **EXPLORING QUESTIONS FOR DISCUSSION**
1. Have you experienced a re-birth . . . a new perspective . . . a fresh start?
2. Where have these experiences taken you? What have you learned about you? What have you learned about God?

• **RELATED SCRIPTURE SOURCES**
> John 3:1-21

• **NEW PERSPECTIVES**
Consider personal changes you can make and/or new steps you can take to be of service to others.

• **QUESTIONS TO BE RESOLVED**
(Can be listed on a separate page)

• **A PRAYER THOUGHT**

"When we were dead in our sins, God made us alive with Christ. He forgave us all our sins, having canceled the written cod, with its regulations, which was against us and which stood opposed to us; He took it away, nailing it to the cross.

Since we have been raised with Christ, let us set our hearts on things above, where Christ is seated at the right hand of God."

WHAT WILL YOU FIND
AT CHRISTMAS?

This week I came across an imaginative and stimulating letter to Santa. A little boy, hoping to get special consideration for Christmas gifts, wrote a letter to Santa Claus that said "Dear Santa, there are three boys living at my house. Jeffrey is two. David is four and Norman is seven. Jeffrey is good some of the time. David is good some of the time, and Norman is good all of the time. I am Norman." That kind of letter is bound to bring special results.

What will you find at Christmas? I want to suggest that you will find what you are looking for.

Every once in a while you experience something that changes you forever. A few weeks ago it happened to me in a rather unsuspecting way and it all happened in church. A worship service can usually move along in a predictable pattern. In the bulletin I noticed in the middle of the order of worship a sentence which said, "A Personal Testimony."

When we came to that part of the service, the pastor invited a parishioner in the rear of the sanctuary to come forward to speak. She rose out of her custom-made motorized wheelchair, and walked briskly to the front of the sanctuary where she extended her arms high above her head and exclaimed with excitement her joy and thanksgiving to God for healing from viral encephalitis and six and one-half years of almost complete crippling physical and mental handicaps. This forty-five year old woman was someone we all observed for more than six years, deteriorating from a vital active person to one who could no longer walk, struggled with slurred speech, and suffered with growing deficits in her pattern of thinking.

She came regularly to worship assisted by her automated wheelchair. While she was remembered in the weekly congregational prayers and provided with an anointing for healing, this transformation came as a surprise to her and all who knew her. She has experienced a miracle. No eye was dry that Sunday morning, and the experience has had a profound effect on everyone present.

For a lifetime, I have read of Jesus healing a variety of affected human beings a long time ago. But this gift of divine intervention has created a new sense of awe and astonishment in me. What a gift! A new sense of the sacred has been inspired in me!

Some fairly recent issues of Times, Life, Newsweek, and U.S. News and World Report have featured cover stories addressing Christmas. A Newsweek article, entitled "The Search for the Sacred," says this: "Maybe it's just a critical mass of Baby Boomers in the contemplative afternoon of life . . . or maybe it's a general dissatisfaction with the materialism of the modern world. For these reasons and more, millions of Americans are embarking on a search for the sacred in their lives."

People all around us are asking, "Is there any meaning to my life? Does my life count? Is there a God? And if there is a God, can I get to know Him?" That's what Christmas is all about – getting to know God.

We all have a natural thirst to know God. God knows all about you and me. He wants us to know Him. And there is no better time than Christmas to become the kind of seeker the Wise Men embodied.

Wise people still seek Christ. The miracle of Christmas is not on 34th Street, it is in Bethlehem. It's in our hearts and God offers us forgiveness for our past, peace of mind in the present, and a solid future in eternity. It's time to unwrap the gift.

WHAT WILL YOU FIND AT CHRISTMAS?
REFLECTION/QUEST TIME

• EXPLORING QUESTIONS FOR DISCUSSION
1. Are you embarked on a search for the sacred in your life? Where are you looking? What specific steps are you taking?
2. Does the Wisemen's search for Jesus give you any clues? (Matthew 2:7-12)
3. If Christmas is all about getting to know God, are you ready to unwrap the gift?

• RELATED SCRIPTURE SOURCES
Matthew 2:7-12

• NEW PERSPECTIVES
Consider personal changes you can make and/or new steps you can take to be of service to others.

• QUESTIONS TO BE RESOLVED
(Can be listed on a separate page)

• A PRAYER THOUGHT

"By the tender mercy of our God, the dawn from on high has broken upon us, to give light to those who sit in darkness and in the shadow of death.

To guide our feet into the way of peace.

For unto us a Child is born,

Unto us a Son is given.

God so loved the world that He gave His only Son, so that everyone who believes in Him may not perish but may have eternal life. Indeed, God did not send the Son into the world to condemn the world, but in order that the world might be saved through Him.

Thanks be to God for this gift beyond words!"

RECEIVE THE GIFT OF PEACE

At the moment, as each of us lives on the edge of turmoil, the most reassuring gift we seek is peace. The psalmist commented that "Great peace have those who love Your law." (Psalms 119:165) Peace is a word that our world uses a lot, but most people do not have the foggiest idea what it truly means.

For many, peace of mind means drinking until they are so drunk and numb that they can no longer feel the pain in their hearts.

For some, peace remains hopping from one relationship to the next, to the next, and to the next, hoping that somebody will fill the void in their lives. But nobody ever does.

For some, peace means staying busy all the time so that at night they just collapse into bed and don't have to think. Because any time that they are quiet, those haunting thoughts, those fears, and that terrible loneliness comes caving in. They can't stand that feeling.

For other people, peace means working and working; becoming a workaholic and overachieving, so they can get all the attributes of success to prove to the world that they are somebody! But inside they are saying "I don't really feel like somebody."

For others, peace means trying New Age gimmicks, like gazing at crystals or relying on aromatherapy to cure their ills. But that is not peace of mind either.

Real peace of mind is having a relationship with Jesus Christ, and becoming friends with God.

Real peace is knowing no matter what I do, God will never stop loving me.

Real peace is knowing no matter what happens, even in a time of terrorism and war, God will never leave me alone. He will always be with me.

Real peace means no matter what happens this year, or in the years to come, I know that God is going to give me strength to handle it.

Real peace is living with God's Word, the Bible, so that I can avoid a lot of needless hang-ups and hurts and habits that mess up my life.

Real peace is teaching my children God's Word as a foundation for life, so that when I see them making certain decisions, I can say, "Boy, I'm proud of that! I wasn't even there, and my kids made that decision on their own." That's real peace.

There are things that rob us of peace of mind: guilt, grief, and grudges. The Christmas message is that God sent a Savior to wipe away our sins in order that we can be forgiven. Jesus gives us a clear conscience. Without this cleansing, guilt robs us of peace. Grief also robs us. You may be in major pain right now, because life can recreate all kinds of hurtful memories. You may remember the loss of an especially dear loved one, a parent who abandoned you, or a divorce you went through. You have grief that robs you of joy and peace of mind.

God cares about your hurt. God sees it, and He knows all about it. You were never meant to carry that grief all on your own. Never! God says to cast all your cares upon Him and He will care for you. Receive the gift of peace.

There are grudges – grudges that rob us of peace. Grudges cause us to be resentful. You and I will be hurt in life, whether intentionally or unintentionally. How you and I respond to that hurt will determine our happiness in life. For your own peace of mind, let go of those hurts.

That is why we need Jesus Christ, because only He can give us the power to let go. You can find peace of mind, which passes all understanding, if you let God do it God's way. In this season of Lent, it is time to focus on the "man of suffering" who "was acquainted with infirmity" for in Him God promises us forgiveness, peace of mind, and eternal life. (Isaiah 53:3)

RECEIVE THE GIFT OF PEACE
REFLECTION/QUEST TIME

- **EXPLORING QUESTIONS FOR DISCUSSION**
1. Are you hurting? How and why?
2. God promises peace to those who are in relationship with Him. How would you describe that relationship?
3. What spiritual practices could bring you peace?

- **RELATED SCRIPTURE SOURCES**
  Psalm 119:105   I Peter 5:7
  Ephesians 4:19-21   John 14:25-27
  Colossians 3:12-17

- **NEW PERSPECTIVES**
Consider personal changes you can make and/or new steps you can take to be of service to others.

- **QUESTIONS TO BE RESOLVED**
(Can be listed on a separate page)

- **A PRAYER THOUGHT**
"Let the peace of Christ rule in our hearts, since as members of one body we were called to peace. And let us be thankful.

Let the word of Christ dwell in us richly as we teach and admonish one another with all wisdom. Whatever we do, therefore, whether in word or deed, let us do it all in the Name of the Lord Jesus, giving thanks to God the Father through Him."

CATCHING THE
SPIRIT OF FAITH

Once again I have had the privilege of visiting the Flower Show in Philadelphia. The physical grandness of this year's Philadelphia Flower Show is startling. The Pennsylvania Convention Center, a structure that spans two city blocks and contains exhibit halls the size of several football fields, now contains a Flower Show one-and-a-half times larger than it has ever been. After a hard winter, there is nothing more invigorating to stimulate the promise of spring and the joys found in the miracles of new floral life and growth. The Flower Show with the theme "This Land Is Your Land" couldn't come at a better time.

All of us benefit from seeing seed thoughts and ventured risks translated into beautiful realities. The gardens and landscapes elegantly modeled in the Show will undoubtedly inspire thousands more to be attempted among homes and estates in the weeks and months ahead because people caught the dream of pursuing a risky promise. Planting a garden or growing a flower is an adventure loaded equally with risk and promise. But to enjoy the beauty we need to make the journey.

This season of Lent comes to us as a break following a long winter, motivating anyone who seeks to embark on a journey of faith. We capture the atmosphere for claiming new adventures in our spiritual journey in the basic definition of faith found in Biblical description, "Now faith is the assurance of things hoped for, the conviction of things not seen." (Hebrews 11:1)

One man suggested recently that "faith is stupid! It doesn't make sense." There is no guarantee that in our leap of faith we will land successfully on the other side. The metaphor of journey or sojourn is a radical one. It is a challenge to the dominant ideologies of our time, which yearn for settlement, security, and placement. Perhaps this is a reason why the Lenten season has become for so many a time to be avoided.

Speaking about faith in this reflective season portrays Christian discipleship as a following of "the way." (Matthew 8:22; 9:9; 10:38) The "way" as a metaphor is not precisely characterized, but it is variously the way of Jesus, the way of the cross, the way of suffering, and the way to Jerusalem. The term marks Christians as those who live in a way contrasted to every fixed and settled form of life. It is a journey. It is a leap. It may be stupid. It may not make sense.

The journey is modeled. Abram is one of the great Old Testament figures whose shadow is also cast over the whole New Testament. Scripture places special emphasis on his faith life. The basis of his faith was "revelation." The Lord said to him, "Go from your country and kindred and your father's house to the land that I will show you." (Genesis 12:1)

Abram made a life-changing decision to trust and obey. God's promised him that He would provide dramatic fulfillments of his faith: "I will make you a great nation and I will bless you, and make your name great, so that you will be a blessing." (Genesis 12:2)

The man who was to become a great nation could not, at the time, be the father of just one child. But God promised! To a man embarking on a perilous journey that involved famine and threats to his life, God promised unique support and encouragement. Abram arrived at the necessary conclusion, "that what He had promised He was able to perform." (Romans 4:2, KJV)

All of God's children are expected to walk by faith. In this highly mobile society in which we live today, people move because they prefer the climate, or they have a chance at promotion, or they felt a change of environment may solve some of their problems. It may be healthy for us to consider whether we have ever made a move in faith based on what God has been saying to us about His eternal purposes and the role He expects us to play in their fulfillment. Are we ready as we pause in the shadow of the cross to pursue a risky promise? For God's sake, let us begin the journey of faith and claim the promise.

CATCHING THE SPIRIT OF FAITH
REFLECTION/QUEST TIME

• EXPLORING QUESTIONS FOR DISCUSSION
1. What do you believe about life and death, God and Jesus?
2. How would you describe your faith? Are you claiming God's promise for the journey?
3. What convictions/beliefs does your life walk convey to others?

• RELATED SCRIPTURE SOURCES

Hebrews 11:1	Matthew 8:22; 9:9; 10:38
Genesis 12: 1-3	Romans 4:2

• NEW PERSPECTIVES
Consider personal changes you can make and/or new steps you can take to be of service to others.

• QUESTIONS TO BE RESOLVED
(Can be listed on a separate page)

• A PRAYER THOUGHT

"Throughout this Lenten journey, let us keep our eyes fixed on Jesus, the pioneer and perfecter of our faith, Who for the joy that was set before Him endured the cross, disregarding its shame, and has taken His seat at the right hand of the throne of God.

We thank you, Lord Jesus, not only for the privilege of believing in You, but of suffering for You as well, so that we may also be glorified with You."

THE MEANING OF
CHRIST'S CROSS AND OURS

We have had a record winter in terms of snow level, duration of cold temperatures, and dreaded cabin fever. Add to this the misery of leaky roofs, cancellations, stuck cars, and bones broken in falls on icy terrain and people begin to feel sorry for themselves. They long for sunshine and warmth. Essentially we feel punished if not awestruck by the power of the mighty snowflake.

During one of the storms when I was confined indoors, I pulled out a copy of the newspaper from Fargo, North Dakota, where I experienced winter's brutality a few years ago. I reminisced as I read the headlines again: "-100° chill factor, Record of the Century." I remember bringing home this newspaper with its caption, in order to be able to document to my wife what severe conditions I had endured.

During a week of travel and programs at the Moravian churches of North Dakota, I also learned about and experienced a new term they used called "Snirt." This was a mixture of snow and dirt, which blew across the plains in razor-like fashion to sting and cut exposed portions of a person's skin. The brave people of that region know what real winters are all about, and endure them with a sense of acceptance and challenge.

When life delivers to any one of us personally what seems to be wintry blasts of trials, pain, or disappointments, we tend to feel "put upon." It is not unusual to hear someone say this is their "cross to bear."

We need to make a distinction between what we consider to be needless pain or inconvenience, and what Jesus means when He said "If any want to become my followers, let them deny themselves, and take up their cross and follow Me. For those who want to save their life will lose it, and those who lose their life for My sake, and for the sake of the Gospel, will save it." (Mark 8:34-35)

This one statement is the essence of what this Lenten season should be all about. We are given the opportunity to confront firsthand the meaning of Christ's cross and ours.

Jesus used carrying a cross to illustrate the ultimate submission required of His followers. He is not against pleasure, nor is He saying that we should seek pain needlessly. He is talking about the heroic effort needed to follow Him moment by moment, to do His will when the work of life is difficult and the future looks bleak.

Jesus wants us to choose to follow Him rather than a life of sin and self-satisfaction. He wants us to stop trying to control our destiny and to let Him direct us. He asks for submission, not self-hatred. He asks us only to lose our self-centered determination to be in charge. Pleasure, possessions, position, and power are ultimately worthless. They are temporary. They cannot be exchanged for our soul.

Jesus gives us a choice: choosing the cross, he reminds us, is a matter of saving, not losing.

The Meaning of Christ's Cross and Ours
Reflection/Quest Time

• Exploring Questions for Discussion
1. Does carrying the cross alert us to lose our self-centered determination to be in charge?
2. What does it mean to follow Christ moment by moment, and do His will when the work of life is difficult and the future looks bleak?
3. How do you explain in contemporary understanding Jesus' statement, "those who want to save their life will lose it, and those who lose their life for My sake, for the sake of the Gospel will save it?"

• Related Scripture Sources
Mark 8:34-35

• New Perspectives
Consider personal changes you can make and/or new steps you can take to be of service to others.

• Questions to be Resolved
(Can be listed on a separate page)

• A Prayer Thought

"Lord God, Son, the Savior of the world, though You were in the form of God, You did not consider equality with God something to cling to, but emptied Yourself, taking the form of a servant, being born in human likeness. You humbled Yourself and became obedient to the point of death, even death on a cross.

Your love compels us to live not for ourselves, but for You."

HOPE IN THE
FACE OF DIFFICULTY

This is Good Friday, and Easter is coming. What does this all mean? These two central features of the Christian faith are expressed in so many different ways and rituals. One of the most recent translations of the Bible in contemporary language, *The Message* by Eugene Peterson, sums up these moments in stating: "Our firm decision is to work from this focused center. One man died for everyone. That puts everyone in the same boat. He included everyone in His death so that everyone could also be included in His life, a resurrected life, a far better life than people ever lived on their own." (1 Corinthians 5:14-15)

Among the area observances of Easter during the past 250 years is the announcement of the dawn by various brass choirs of the Moravian Church. Every year, for the past 28 years, instrumental groups have stopped in front of our residence around 4 a.m. to play their festive chorales which conclude as they lead worshippers to the cemetery for the Easter dawn service.

For our family, these early morning musical visits have been a source of joy, although it is highly possible that not every neighbor enjoys these brass interruptions with the same enthusiasm. Here in Nazareth, some of our neighbors join with our family to have coffee, hot chocolate, and Moravian sugar cake, to warm the spirits of these musical troubadours.

Some years ago, as my wife and I served a Moravian parish in semi-rural Ohio, our brass choir traveled to neighborhood centers to play Easter hymns at early hours. One of the new stops on the schedule that year was in front of the home of one supermarket owner who was unfamiliar with this Easter tradition. The next day, on Easter Monday, I visited his store and heard his voice bellowing from behind his meat counter to his check-out clerk at the front of the store.

He called to her and said, "Alice, you will never believe what we experienced on early Easter dawn in our neighborhood."

"What was that, Mr. Stanley?" the cashier replied.

"Some drunken German band stopped in a truck in front of our house and played their polka. What a way to start a new day!" the owner remarked.

I chuckled to myself. The tradition goes on. So does the truth which Good Friday and Easter represent.

Jesus suffered immensely on the cross, even to the point of feeling abandonment when He exclaimed "My God, why have You forsaken me?" Suffering and disappointments are our common lot. We are unrealistic if we think these befall only "the unfortunate." Suffering befalls all of us, even though the form of suffering and difficulty undoubtedly is different for varying groups of people.

Some difficulties are clearly of our own making. For these we need to assume personal responsibility. Our quest must be to move from difficulty to hope. We need to mobilize our pain and not waste our sorrows; we need to transform our despair into signs of hope. While this transformation may not always result in the hoped for solution, it can always lead to greater hope and faith – a hope that continues to choose life; a hope that actively resists evil; a hope that sees beyond the personal and carries the birth pangs of the new order; a hope that sustains us in the face of difficulty.

St. Paul in his letter to the church in Corinth said it so well: "So we're not giving up. How could we! Even though on the outside it looks like things are falling apart on us, in the inside, where God is making new life, not a day goes by without His unfolding grace. These hard times are small potatoes compared to the good times, the lavish celebration prepared for us. There's far more here than meets the eyes. The things we see now are here today, gone tomorrow. But the things we can't see now will last forever." (2 Corinthians 4:16-18, *The Message*)

Hope in the Face of Difficulty
Reflection/Quest Time

- **Exploring Questions for Discussion**
1. Despite suffering, difficulty, and disappointment as our common lot, spiritually speaking, how can a resurrected life in Christ lead to a far better life than people ever achieve of their own?
2. In what ways can Christ's death and resurrection be translated so that you no longer live for yourself but for Him?
3. How can the Spirit give us a guarantee, so we don't lose heart?

- **Related Scripture Sources**
   2 Corinthians 4:7-18
   2 Corinthians 5:1-21

- **New Perspectives**
Consider personal changes you can make and/or new steps you can take to be of service to others.

- **Questions to be Resolved**
(Can be listed on a separate page)

- **A Prayer Thought**

"Easter triumph, Easter joy! This alone can sin destroy;
From sin's power, Lord set us free, newborn souls in You to be.
Al-le-lu-la!"

SPIRITUAL DEATH IS GRADUAL IN UNSUSPECTING WAYS

When Clare Booth Luce was appointed United States Ambassador to Italy, she established residence in a beautiful 17th Century villa. Soon her health began to deteriorate. She lost weight. She had little energy. Her doctors discovered that she was suffering from arsenic poisoning, but the source of the deadly substance remained a mystery until they finally traced it to the ceiling of her bedroom. Some beautiful rose designs, ornately done in bas relief, had been painted with a paint that contained arsenic lead. A fine dust fell from those roses. Mrs. Luce was slowly being poisoned as she lay in her bed.

Physical as well as spiritual death can seize its victims in gradual and unsuspecting ways. Individual acts we call sins can accumulate into a composite pile of spiritual and human debris, when the marred relationship with God continues unnoticed or ignored. In today's world, we are experiencing this gradual poisoning as a nation and as individuals.

As an example, at least two observations of America can and are being made by thoughtful observers: One is that we are the greatest nation in the world. The other is that our culture is in decline.

The second observation is the one which is gripping the consciousness of our nation. Sample indicators of decline show up recently on two covers of Newsweek magazine. The caption on one cover states, "Growing-Up Scared – How Our Kids Are Robbed of Their Childhood." The following week another cover featured the anguished skater, Nancy Kerrigan, exclaiming, "Why Me? - The New Fear of Stalking."

Too long we have accepted with complacency the presence and portrayal of violence and sex on TV, theater screens, and in rock and rap; also, in our social and political maneuverings. Cultural decline, once seen as a gradual development, is now perceived in avalanche proportions.

One perceptive individual, who is seeking to provide a response to our moral decline, is William J. Bennett, the former Secretary of Education and Drug Czar. I have been reading his well-known book, The Book of Virtues. He has collected hundreds of stories in an instructive and inspiring anthology that will help children understand and develop character – and help adults teach them.

Bible stories, exemplary stories from history, great poetry, memorable fables, and elements of Greek mythology and philosophy are all included in Bennett's book. Robert Coles in speaking about this book, called it "wonderfully suggestive, inspiring literature, hums with moral energy . . . a carefully selected collection that fills an aching void in this secular society." I agree. I have even read some portions to my grandchildren to begin the process. The themes of responsibility, courage, compassion, loyalty, honesty, friendship, persistence, hard-work, self discipline, and faith are all in Bennett's book.

Margaret Thatcher, former Prime Minister of England, said that "there is little hope for our countries if the hearts of men and women in democratic societies cannot be touched by a call to something greater than themselves."

One of the themes of the Epiphany season is narrated in the Gospel of Mark (1:14-20), describing the beginning of Jesus' public ministry in His preaching of the coming of the reign of God. His is a call to something greater than ourselves, which begins with a sense of sorrow for our sins and a change of heart.

We all need to meet the call of God to repent and believe. We need to turn from old worn out paths and tired experiments and get back into the basics of morality and character. This is our opportunity to believe the promise of God that is good news. It is God who promises even for times of deep crisis, "See, I make all things new." (Revelation 21:5)

Spiritual Death is Gradual
in Unsuspecting Ways
Reflection/Quest Time

• **Exploring Questions for Discussion**
1. What can each of us do to reverse our cultural decline? Be specific.
2. Is complacency in our attitude toward sin a critical issue in dealing with noticeable decline? Where do we start?
3. Are the passages found in Mark 1:14-20 a call to something greater than ourselves?

• **Related Scripture Sources**

Mark 1:14-20   Revelation 21:5-7

• **New Perspectives**

Consider personal changes you can make and/or new steps you can take to be of service to others.

• **Questions to be Resolved**

(Can be listed on a separate page)

• **A Prayer Thought**

"With sincere hearts and open minds, let us now acknowledge the sin that entangles us and prevents us from doing God's will.

Compassionate Lord, You call us to a higher standard than we have achieved. We therefore bow in honest confession of those thoughts, words, and deeds which have missed the mark. Within our families, we have loved imperfectly. Among sisters and brothers in the church, we have not fully walked in the light. Often our congregations have not reflected the rich diversity of people in our communities. In our witness to the world, our lives have not adequately testified to Your redeeming power. Forgive us, gracious Lord, for permitting ourselves to be distracted from the goal of our discipleship. Heal the brokenness of our hearts and restore us to You, our first love."

YOU'LL NEVER WALK ALONE

The New Year is launched. We have bid farewell to a year in which we were introduced to the dark night of our soul, and as a nation we became aware of a deep rip in the meaning of our existence and our purpose as a people. Hopefully we are embarked on a new stage of openness and commitment to be healers and architects on a bleeding globe which gravely needs samples of resolve, integrity, compassion, good will, and hope.

We need a picture of a new world. This new year is a call for a wider imagination. It takes a large imagination for us to imagine the world as a place where God can reign. In your own experience, think of those times when you, too, easily accepted the world's definition of reality, when you too quickly accommodated to the world's idea of what is possible and permissible. What vision, what gift of new insight enabled you to see something you had previously not seen? What is needed is a vision, some picture of a world other than what we've got. This is a time to speak forth and to offer an alternative image of the world.

When I was in high school in the dark days of 1941, there were dark clouds of war. The outlook was bleak. White chalk cliffs of Dover on the English Channel coast were guideposts for the German plans that flew in a seemingly endless stream to bomb London and other island targets. At the height of the Battle of Briton, the skies above the cliffs held only terror for the British and their Allies. But Nat Burton and Walter Kent, two American songwriters, looked ahead to better days, when the bomber would be replaced by bluebirds and created one of the most touching and beautiful of the "stiff upper lip" songs to come out of World War II.

One of my classmates, Gary Rowland, sang each year at the famous and popular Vocational-Tech Minstrels. Gary was handsome and impressive as he stood on the stage, night after night of the minstrels, to sing this new but visionary song of hope. He supported his body with a crutch that replaced a missing leg lost to an encroaching and ultimately terminal disease. He sang in his mellow voice with a vibrancy that suggested an unknown tomorrow, when peace and freedom would abound. Each evening that he sang, tears and applause called him back for a series of encores. He left such an indelible impression on me. So much so, that at a later date I awakened early one morning on my trip home from serving in Europe and Africa, to go to the deck of my ship to take photos of those white cliffs of Dover. Those photos provide treasured inspiration. Those words he sang rang out:

There'll be bluebirds over
The white cliffs of Dover,
Tomorrow, just you wait and see.
There'll be love and laughter
And peace ever after,
Tomorrow, when the world is free.

The shepherd will tend his sheep;
The valley will bloom again;
And Jimmy will go to sleep
In his own little room again.
There'll be bluebirds over
The white cliffs of Dover,
Tomorrow, just you wait and see.

Something is afoot in our everyday world. We have the makings of a transformed world opened up, made new by the incursion of a living God in Christ.
God who indicates that He makes "all things new" was the inspiration of the
Wisemen, who in this season of Epiphany, known in the church as the season of
the Star, exalted the truth that "the Word became human and lives with us." We
are encouraged to sing to the Lord a new song for God does marvelous things
today and tomorrow, just you wait and see.

We are guided by the Star of Bethlehem, illumined by its light, even in the
darkest night. Richard Rodgers caught this in the musical "Carousel" endowed
with spirituality and climactic intensity when he wrote "You'll Never Walk
Alone." Its message is one of hope.

When you walk through a storm hold your head up high
And don't be afraid of the dark.
At the end of the storm is a golden sky
And sweet silver song of a lark.
Walk on through the wind.
Walk on through the rain,
Though your dreams be tossed and blown.
Walk on, walk on, with hope in your heart
And you'll never walk alone.
You'll never walk alone.

This season of Epiphany attempts to speak of a reality beyond our present realities, that time when God gets God's way with the world. Do we have eyes to see that world coming to be among us? Have we some imagination to comprehend the width, depth, and breadth of a new tomorrow placed before the people of God? In faith, we never need to walk alone.

You'll Never Walk Alone
Reflection/Quest Time

> **• Exploring Questions for Discussion**
> 1. We are in need of openness and commitment to be healers and architects on a bleeding globe. Can you identify in people or recent events examples of resolve, integrity, compassion, good will, and hope? Does this challenge motivate an inward call in you to serve?
> 2. Are you hopeful that God's love will ultimately triumph? What role can you play in the transformation of the world?
> 3. Who or what is most often your walking companion? Have you felt the presence of God? Have you invited Jesus? Be diligent in your search for the Star.

• Related Scripture Sources
    Matthew 2:1-12

• New Perspectives
Consider personal changes you can make and/or new steps you can take to be of service to others.

• Questions to be Resolved
(Can be listed on a separate page)

> **• A Prayer Thought**
>
> "All Your creatures, Lord, will praise You, and all Your people will give You thanks.
>
> They will speak of the glory of Your royal power and tell of Your might.
>
> Everyone will know Your mighty deeds and the glorious majesty of Your kingdom.
>
> Your rule is eternal, and You are King forever.
>
> You, Lord, are righteous in all You do, merciful in all Your acts.
>
> You are near to those who call to You, who call to You with sincerity."

THE POWER
OF THE SPIRITUAL BIRTH

Everybody knows that there are times when a person outdoes him/herself. As one who plays tennis at least once a week throughout the year, I am aware that every now and then, on an unpredictable day, the tennis game goes particularly well. A tennis partner can usually be heard to say, "I didn't think you had it in you."

A young football player, for instance, in the last two minutes of the game as his team in losing, makes a touchdown. He runs faster than his legs can carry him, and farther than he dreamed of running.

When he comes out, the coach says to him, "I didn't know you had it in you."

He replies, "I didn't. I was picked up and carried by something outside myself."

That is the experience that people have when they completely outreach and outdo themselves. That is what Pentecost is all about – the day and the season which the Christian church is now observing as the birth of the church.

The birth event is described by the writer of the book of Acts in the Bible in a single sentence, "All of them were filled with the Holy Spirit and began to speak in other languages, as the Spirit gave them ability." (Acts 2:4) It was a unifying experience which transcended all barriers of nationality and language. We might call it "the divine disturbance." Clearly the Spirit of God overtook these simple believers with unusual power. They were not aware of an earlier reminder declaring that, "It is not for you to know the times and or periods that the Father has set by His own authority." (Acts 1:7)

The birth of the church involved a small group of the followers of Jesus. They were talking in a very unusual way. Their passionate conviction conveyed the power of their message even to others who did not understand their language. They were unusually fearless.

Every now and again, the Spirit breaks through into this world of flesh and matter in an incredibly wonderful way. Into a degenerate Roman world, where there seemed to be no hope for any good future, came a mighty rushing wind and flames of fire, like a directive from on high. All the things people though were fixed forever changed, and a free, life-renewing Spirit invaded this world from the outside.

The question therefore is: Is Pentecost reproducible?

There are two things that invariably draw people together: a common danger and a common devotion. Danger drives them together. Devotion draws them together. They come together voluntarily, and therefore those who do not have the will are left out. The purpose of the Pentecostal experience is to enable people to feel the reality and power of the unseen and the spiritual; to offset the overemphasis on the material things of life.

We are living in a time of general uneasiness, sensing troublesome inroads of moral decay and potential chaos in this country and around the world. In a world in which it is possible for the Spirit to work such mighty acts, what is preventing it now? What is in us that is blocking it? Perhaps more than ever we need to hear again a first century message, "Everyone who calls on the name of the Lord will be saved." (Acts 2:21)

THE POWER OF THE SPIRITUAL BIRTH
REFLECTION/QUEST TIME

• **EXPLORING QUESTIONS FOR DISCUSSION**
1. Have you learned to offset the material things of life?
2. How might you experience "the unseen"?
3. Is Pentecost reproducible? How?

• **RELATED SCRIPTURE SOURCES**

Acts 1:7-8   Acts 2:21

Acts 2:4

• **NEW PERSPECTIVES**

Consider personal changes you can make and/or new steps you can take to be of service to others.

• **QUESTIONS TO BE RESOLVED**

(Can be listed on a separate page)

• A PRAYER THOUGHT

"We believe God's promise in these last days. I will pour out my Spirit upon all flesh, and your sons and your daughters shall prophesy; your young men shall see visions, and your old men shall dream dreams. Upon both men and women in those days I will pour out My Spirit; and they shall speak My message.

The spirit of God swells in us if we belong to Christ. The Spirit bears witness with our spirit that we are children of God, and if children, their heirs, heirs of God and joint heirs with Christ.

When the Holy Spirit comes upon us, we receive power, and we become God's witnesses.

The fruit that the Spirit brings to the lives of those who follow Christ is love, joy, peace, patience, kindness, generosity, faithfulness, gentleness, and self control.

The diverse and empowering gifts of the Spirit are given to each one for the common good. None of us is useless to God. None of us is sufficient alone. We serve through the body of Christ, and we depend on the people of Christ."

VISION OF THE POSSIBLE

Gracious God
of love and hope,
vision of what is possible,
Transcender of limits,
always birthing hope,
within, beyond:

We thank You for Your presence
and love,
for the touch of Your hand
on the places of pain.

We are so thankful that You lived
and experienced our life,
experienced our limits,
and know our struggle.

Whatever our difficulties
we celebrate life
and open our hearts to
Your companionship.
We are amazed at
all that
meets us:
hope and love.

Our hand in Yours,
we follow where we
are not sure
except of You.

Ultimately
You make the difference
in Your presence and love,
the touch expressed
in the many dimensions
of Your hand and heart.

– Art Freeman

Notes Worth Taking

NOTES WORTH TAKING

– SUPPORT TEAM –

L-R: Randy, son; Mary, wife; Bill Matz Sr., author; Donna Becker, print composer and designer; Bill Jr., son; and Carol Feilbach Olzinski, editor.

AUTHOR'S AFTERWORD

Your comments are welcome and can be sent to:

wilmarmatz@verizon.net

– Bill Matz

Made in the USA
Charleston, SC
16 January 2010